Title | The Perfect Pizza Dough
Subtitle | Pizza as a profession
Author | Fabrizio Casucci

Photography
Hillina Fradellin's photos
Hillina Fradellin's cover photo
Photos provided by Marana Forni in the baking chapter

ISBN | 978-88-31672-71-9

Youcanprint Self-Publishing
Via Roma, 73 - 73039 Tricase (LE) - Italy
www.youcanprint.it
info@youcanprint.it
Facebook: facebook.com/youcanprint.it
Twitter: twitter.com/youcanprintit

THE PERFECT

PIZZA

DOUGH

Pizza as a profession

FABRIZIO CASUCCI

I have personally translated and adapted this book for the global market, though I am aware of the fact, that my English is very basic, hence, my choice comes from the desire to convey the fundamental concepts to everyone, making them easy and simple to understand, I am sure you will forgive my English.
In order to improve yourself, to learn new methods or to confirm what you are already doing, I sincerely hope you will find all what you are looking for in this text and that you may profitably apply and use it at work.

Time, a sheer passion, experimentation, and application, is necessary to write any technical books on pizza; if the reading will be useful to you, to your liking and able to develop a positive review, this would be a great support and will be much appreciated.

For consultations, you may contact me at the following email address
lapizzaeunarte@gmail.com

Follow me on

 *https://www.facebook.com/lapizzaeunarte*

 *Instagram: Fabrizio.Casucci*

FABRIZIO.CASUCCI

Preface

Commitment, passion, study, and research have pushed me to translate this text into English, aimed to make the world aware of techniques used by Masters Pizzaioli like myself and whoever shows to care about Pizza as a high-quality product.
The dough is undoubtedly the most important element and must be made by respecting fundamental steps; at first, its maturation, considered to be a key and an essential point of its production process; maturation must be combined with the working method, the raw material and much more.
But why is maturation so important? Because it is the result of enzymatic hydrolysis, a process carried out by enzymes reducing complex parts into simpler and more easily digestible components.
The book is enriched with a digestibility theory based on weaker flours which, when used with certain precautions, could well provide a more digestible as well as an excellent quality product. Indirect dough methods, Biga and Poolish, cold technique, the correct use of mixes of different flours are some of the points we will see.

Summary

THE PERFECT PIZZA DOUGH

choose carefully the type of product you desire

apply the right maturation

carefully choose the right flour for the chosen working method

choose which dough method you would like to apply

decide the most suitable processing method for the chosen maturation type

direct dough method,or indirect dough method, that includes the preferment biga or poolish

THE PERFECT PIZZA DOUGH Pizza as a profession

A dough is made up with flour, water, yeast, salt and lipids, which are not essentials for its making, despite the fact they do play a very important role in the whole process.

What should a dough must have to become so special?

If one looks at the organization chart on the previous page, one may notice that I started by identifying the desired product, in reality, all the following points are to be evaluated together, this is because they are linked to each other, for example, I cannot use a weak flour and proceed with an indirect dough method, nor hydrating a weak flour at 80%, nor using a very strong flour for a leavening for example, for 4 or 6 hours.

Having said that, besides the choice of the product, the type of dough, the type of flour, we have a point that remains firm and is related to the <u>maturation of the dough.</u>

The maturation of the dough is not always considered a topic, whether you are working in a pizzeria, as a hobby or a passion at home.

We often hear about long leavening, but this term is not really correct and let's take a look at what I mean.
When we eat pizza, what worries us, besides its taste, is its digestibility or that you may get thirsty, a good dough, must deal with these problems.
But how? With a long leavening? Using a good flour? Using an indirect dough method? We say that an indirect dough is certainly better than a direct dough, as well as an excellent stone-ground and full-body flour is better than a very refined one, but for these things to affect the digestibility of the product, it is necessary to use some very important processing methods.
A dough made with strong flour that has had a long leavening, it is not necessarily better than a dough made with weak flour, which has had a lower leavening time, but that has matured a lot in the fridge cell.
To understand this step, we must necessarily and carefully understand the *maturation concept.*
All flours, strong or less strong, with gluten (an inappropriate term and you will understand why) or gluten-free, almost all contain equal amounts of STARCH, this complex sugar (polysaccharide) is not easy to digest.
To this, we must add, that strong flours and less strong flours differ substantially for the insoluble proteins that are responsible for the formation of gluten, these proteins are not really to be underestimated because of the bonds that are generated, they can, in fact, cause immunological reactions at the intestinal level, something that goes beyond digestibility.
Back to the dough making procedure, what should we do to make it more digestible? We must start to put our thoughts on maturation on whichever product we are going to make.

With the maturation of the Pizza dough, the complex parts are broken down into simpler and more easily digestible parts.

Mixed with 30% Biga, topped with goat ricotta cheese, milk's flower mozzarella, and cherry tomatoes.

I personally made all the pizzas in the pictures, including the dough.

THE MATURATION OF THE DOUGH

Flour, water, yeast, salt, fat, makes our dough, which once is formed, it contains parts that for us are not digestible, but fortunately, the flour also provides us enzymes that are able to break down these indigestible parts to make them easily assimilated by the body.

The maturation process of the dough is the result of enzymatic hydrolysis and is essentially divided into:

Amylolysis   *refers to the process in which amylase enzymes break down starch, a polysaccharide, into simpler components.*

Proteolysis   *refers to the process in which proteolytic enzymes split proteins into peptides.*

Lipolysis   *refers to the process in which lipolytic enzymes break down lipids into glycerol and fatty acids.*

Enzymes are a particular class of proteins and are real biological catalysts, most biological reactions catalyzed by enzymes are millions of times faster than they would be without these catalysts.

Enzymatic hydrolysis is a chemical reaction in which some enzymes break molecular bonds in the presence of water, it is then clear that the amount of hydration of the dough also affects this chemical reaction, which will be more or less accelerated.

A freshly formed dough contains indigestible parts and if it is eaten close to its formation, our digestive system has to make an enormous effort. For this reason, we must ensure that the enzymatic hydrolysis takes place before degustation.

The first element that certainly makes a dough difficult to digest, is the starch, due to its complexity and its very high percentage in the flour (about 70%).

But what is starch? *Starch is a polysaccharide*, a complex sugar: a combination of two polymers of glucose. It is not soluble in water and is the most important source of carbohydrates for human cellular metabolism. Starch is present in large quantities in cereals, then in flours (rice, oats, wheat, corn, barley, etc..), potatoes, bananas and vegetable tissues such as tubers and vegetables.
Starch is an excellent source of carbohydrates for the diet, but above all, it acts as a reserve for the body and this because its splitting occurs slowly.

Dough with buckwheat. Mixes of this type require the technique of autolysis, alternatively, you can stop the machine (stop & go), for at least 20 minutes.

How the maturation of the dough acts on the starch and why it is important

The complex carbohydrates digestion such as starch begins in the oral cavity and continues in the intestine, the so-called, "cleavage process", which transforms polysaccharides into individual monosaccharides allowing the intestinal mucosa, in this way, to absorb them. Basically, this is a process transforming sugar complexes into simple sugars and which eventually do not need to be digested and absorbed. The fact is that digesting starch is not a simple thing and requires a lot of work from our body, which will have to secrete enzymes capable of attacking it and very very slowly start to break it down. We must not forget that there is also resistant starch classified in 4 categories, resistant starch (RS) is not digestible by human salivary and pancreatic enzymes.

Here is where our maturation must intervene, in fact, the enzymes we produce to break down the polysaccharides are also present in the flour (amylase enzymes).

Amylolysis is the transformation of starch into simpler sugars, this process is carried out by **alpha and beta-amylase.**
Alpha and beta-amylase have different roles: alpha is called liquefying enzyme, and beta-amylase is called saccharifying enzyme.

Alpha-amylase degrades the alpha bonds (1-4) and transforms the starch into dextrins which, being soluble in water, increases the volume in the liquid phase of the dough. When there are too many alpha-amylases, the mixture is liquefied and its capacity to absorb liquids is reduced; in other words, if the presence of alpha-amylase is excessive or very active, there is a considerable and rapid production of dextrins which, being soluble, increase the liquid phase by softening and making the mixture moist.

That's why **alpha-amylase** is called **liquefying enzymes**. Anyone who has tried to knead using rye flour completely will have noticed that it produces a very sticky dough, not very tied and with a low capacity to retain carbon dioxide during leavening, all this is due to the high content of alpha-amylase enzymes.

Beta-amylase degrades the alpha (1-4) glycosidic bonds of the outer wall of starch, gradually detaching the maltose (two molecules of glucose), this enzyme is therefore called **saccharifying.**

The maltose obtained is transformed into glucose by the enzyme maltase contained in the yeast and this is one of the reasons why without yeast maturation is not perfectly complete, as some enzymes are present also, or even only, in the yeast and contribute in part to the splitting. In this specific case, however, it is true that maltase is also present in the intestine and pancreas and acts at a point in the chain, where the cleavage is almost complete; moreover, maltose is considered digestible, for this reason, the influence of this enzyme on maturation in terms of digestibility for the body is very minimal.

Unlike alpha-amylases, beta amylases are typical of the plant world, they are produced by many plants but also by fungi and bacteria. Unlike alpha-amylases, beta-amylases are not produced by man, which is why the importance of maturation increases. Beta-amylases are much more selective molecules than alpha-amylases that cut the starch molecules indistinctly. (amylases cannot break healthy starch, they break down only that damaged for example by grinding).

Shape correctly the pizza dough ball is an art, you must not touch the edge and the central part must remain uniform.

The importance of amylolysis on yeast life

Maturation has an effect on the sugars complex splitting into simple sugars, aimed to make the product more digestible; it also has GREAT importance, by providing fermentable sugars for yeasts.

After the amylase enzymes splitting, the sugars present in the dough, are transformed upon disaccharides form, such as maltose and sucrose. However, yeast has a semipermeable membrane and allows only monosaccharides to go through. To transform maltose and sucrose, it uses two enzymes:

The invertase, *which is able to transform the sucrose into the two molecules that compose it: glucose and fructose.*

Maltase *can split the maltose molecule into the two glucose molecules that compose it*

The molecules of glucose and fructose, like monosaccharides, are able to penetrate the yeast cells, where the zymase enzyme, by intervening in glycolysis, give rise to alcoholic fermentation, generating ethyl alcohol and carbon dioxide.

Amylolysis increases the digestibility of the dough and provides nourishment for the yeasts.

Dough loaves from 200 grams up to 220 should be arranged as in the picture, once risen they should touch each other.
The first step enabling you to make a nice pizza is to extract the leavened dough still perfectly round, but if they are all attached this operation is not possible, also, when you cut the dough to divide it, it could easily burn at that point.

Proteolysis

The other element that affects the digestion of the dough is constituted by insoluble proteins (for insoluble proteins see the flour chapter on page 78), insoluble proteins are responsible for the formation of gluten. One of them, Gliadin, is also the cause of celiac disease, which affects intolerant people.
This type of protein is an indicator of the strength of the flour, the famous W, in fact the more these proteins are present, the more the gluten comes out strong and the higher the W value rises (see the chapter on Gluten on page 79).
Proteolysis is the process that takes place through hydrolysis of the peptide bond by enzymes called proteases and for which proteins, partly also those of gluten, are broken down into peptides component. Thanks to the maturation, along with proteolysis, it is possible in part to reduce these proteins to peptides, I mean in part, because some enzymes are not present in the flour, so some bonds cannot be broken down completely.

To be clearer, prolamines, such as wheat gliadin, are rich in proline and glutamine, two hardly digestible amino acids that are part of the category of non-essential amino acids, since the body is able to synthesize them. It is the high content of proline and glutamine present in gluten that prevents complete proteolysis by digestive enzymes and this is why they are not easy to digest, in fact in the digestive tract of man there are no digestive enzymes (prolyl - endopeptidase) capable of cleaves peptide bonds involving this amino acid.

Therefore, the stronger the flours are, the greater the presence of these proteins, which can give rise to immunological reactions after they have "crossed" the gastrointestinal tract. In addition, there is a possibility that disulfide bridges (or disulfide bond) will remain to bind peptides in the proteolytic fragments. The problem is not so much related to digestibility but to possible immunological reactions more or less accentuated depending on the individual, because we cannot ignore the fact that we are not all the same and not all have the same intestinal microflora.

Although the enzyme protease plays an important role in splitting proteins, making the work easier for our bodies, I believe that the use of weaker, selected flours should be taken into serious consideration in order to minimize this problem.

Returning to proteolysis, however, we must pay attention to one detail: it weakens the glutinic mesh, so a long proteolysis makes the dough easier to break during processing, it also creates microholes and, the carbon dioxide produced by the yeasts that are responsible for the swelling of the dough, begins to come out; the result will be a less-developed product.

Lipolysis

Lipolysis is the process by which the fats contained in the dough are broken down into glycerol and fatty acids by the lipase enzyme and then the fatty acids are oxidized to peroxide by the lipoxygenase enzyme.

Lipoxygenase, thanks to its strong oxidative action, tends to develop peroxides, which positively influence gluten by increasing its capacity to absorb water.
The peroxides formed during kneading act on the thiol groups, oxidizing them and transforming them into disulfide groups.

The disulfide groups (-S-S-) have less chance of being attacked by enzymes, the result will be stronger gluten.
Lipoxygenase also has a bleaching effect on the dough through the oxidation of carotenoid pigments (Adrian, Potus, & Frangne, 2009). Soya flour is the richest in lipoxygenase.

I wish to remind in this paragraph, why the wheat germ is removed from the flour: the reactions activated by the enzymes seen here, involve the release of fatty acids and are therefore responsible for the increase in acidity during storage of the flour; to increase its preservation we opt for greater refining, eliminating, in particular, the wheat germ, where the lipids are located and thus prolonging its shelf life.
It is clear that using "raw" flours obtained with stone grinding, there are greater quantities of lipids, consequently with more pronounced lipolysis, precisely because of the greater presence of enzymes and fats.
In wheat, the lipase is mainly located in the bran and germ.

In the past, there were not all these problems of intolerance related to flours, problems that have grown with the coming of genetically modified flours to meet bread makers' needs.

For example, ancient grains; in Italy we have many varieties which did not go under any genetic manipulation, not only, but ancient grains, unlike many other varieties built in the laboratory, need less herbicides treatment, if none at all.

We have to understand that *for a good dough we cannot ignore an excellent raw material, which does not necessarily mean, strong flour.*

I'm concentrating on using less strong flours, possibly cut with regrinded semolina and I'm trying to divert on some ancient grains, even if the Spelt or the Quinoa remains among my favorites (here too, however, depends on their processing and origin).

Dough with 20% Quinoa and Quinoa seeds.
As Quinoa is a gluten-free flour, it should be combined with a flour of strength. Autolysis is used.

As I said before, the steps of the initial organization chart (page 10), are completely linked together, we can not only think of the right technique and the right hydration, we must absolutely choose carefully our raw material, i.e. the flour, combine the right hydration, a perfect maturation and adequate leavening.

If only we consider the flour technical data, the rheological aspects, we evaluate only the product in order to be able to work it easily, while in my opinion, we must also consider the nutritional, health and digestibility aspect.

When we see Pizzaioli widening the pizza loaves making freestyle, throwing it in the air for minutes and this remains perfect, either it is made of rubber or it is made of strong flours, which develop gluten mesh extremely elastic, are you convinced that to see something beautiful could also mean to be digestible?

MATURATION OF THE DOUGH AND COLD TECHNIQUE

Before we tackle this chapter, it is important to learn the broad outlines of how enzymes behave at low temperatures.

The question is what happens to enzymes with cold, to face this step, in my opinion, we need to go to the extreme, i.e. freezing, but to understand how freezing affects enzymatic activity, it is necessary first of all to understand the effect of temperature on the molecules that are the substrates for enzymatic catalysis.

Molecular movement and the role of temperature

All cells are made up of molecules, which in turn are formed by atoms.
In biochemistry, a substrate is defined as a molecule on which an enzyme acts.
Substrates are therefore the starting molecules of catalyzed chemical reactions.
Enzyme reactions depend on the collision of the molecules with the substrate.

Inside the cells, the molecules of the substrate are in constant random motion, known as Brownian motion, with Brownian motion means a disorderly motion of small particles present in fluids or fluid suspensions, a phenomenon discovered by the Scottish botanist Robert Brown and then confirmed by Albert Einstein. This random movement of the molecules is influenced by temperature, which if it increases gives rise to a faster motion with consequent more collisions between molecules and enzymes (kinetic energy increases with temperature).

As the temperature decreases, the opposite effect occurs, i.e. the movement of the molecules and consequently their number of collisions with enzymes decreases.

At the freezing point, there is a crystallization that drastically slows down the molecular movement, the molecules have less freedom of movement than in a liquid solution. Automatically, enzyme-substrate collisions become extremely rare and enzyme activity is almost zero. (Graw, 2018).

However, this happens at the frozen point, which is why the temperature of the cold room must be kept between 3 and 4 °C.

Enzyme reactions are subject to substrate temperature and pH, and of course also to the amount of enzymes present. The pH is another factor of great importance in the splitting processes, although most enzymes work best within a range of 6 to 8, it should not be forgotten that outside the pH values, enzymes lose their shape and undergo denaturation. It is useless to say how many other variables should be added considering specific behaviors of the catalysts still studied by famous biochemists.

One thing remains certain, to obtain a maturation, the cold rooms or the refrigerator must be set between 3 and 4 °C, the temperature at which the enzymes are slow but active.

Understanding the maturation of the dough

Contrary to what you might think, the maturation of the dough begins when we combine water and flour, the yeast has almost no importance in this phase.

Why do I say this? Because if we understand this concept we can opt for different maturation techniques.

The enzymatic processes disregard the presence of yeast, but we must make a consideration about leavening. The advent of strong flours has allowed us to

reach long leavening, yes indeed, because the higher the W, the stronger and more resistant the gluten mesh is and the more it can retain inside the CO_2 produced by the yeast during fermentation. In other words, if we want to leaven a dough out of the fridge at room temperature (19/21gradi) for 16/18 hours we need a very strong flour, we say with a W of at least 350/380, if instead, we opt for leavening of 6/8 hours, it is right to use a flour with a W of about 240/260.
Where is the problem? We must keep in mind that a minimum maturation is at least 24 hours (weak flours) and a good maturation also reaches 48 hours, especially if very strong flours are used.

We immediately notice that we have completely different timing of maturation and leavening, in fact, if a flour holds a maximum leavening of 18 hours how do I let it ferment up to 48 hours to get the right maturation? The answer is simple: you can't! This is because the leavening process is much faster than the maturation process. That's why those who tell me "I make long leavening" don't mean anything to me. Long leavening is not synonymous with a completely mature and therefore digestible product.

Since the final purpose is to obtain a leavened and mature product, we must ensure that the timing between leavening and maturation coincides, otherwise we would obtain a leavened but not ripe pizza (for mature we mean digestible).

Dough with 30% of Biga, to which maturation of 36 hours was applied.

From the dough formation to the pizza loaf preparation, two processes are initiated:

1. Fermentation
2. Enzymatic hydrolysis

Fermentation is relatively fast, enzymatic hydrolysis, on the other hand, takes much longer, but we can slow down or even stop leavening, let's see how: between 3 and 4 °C the yeast is inactive (it does not die) and stops the production of ethyl alcohol and carbon dioxide, enzymes instead at low temperature continue to work even if more slowly.
The solution is to stop or slow down the rising process thanks to the use of cold, bringing our dough to a temperature just below 4 °C to allow the enzymes to continue their work while the yeast is dormant and not active.

The following graphs study the behavior of a dough made with strong flour able to withstand about 20 hours of fermentation. The aim is to make the leavening and maturation behavior comprehensible with and without the use of the cold room.

First case: leavening without the aid of cold

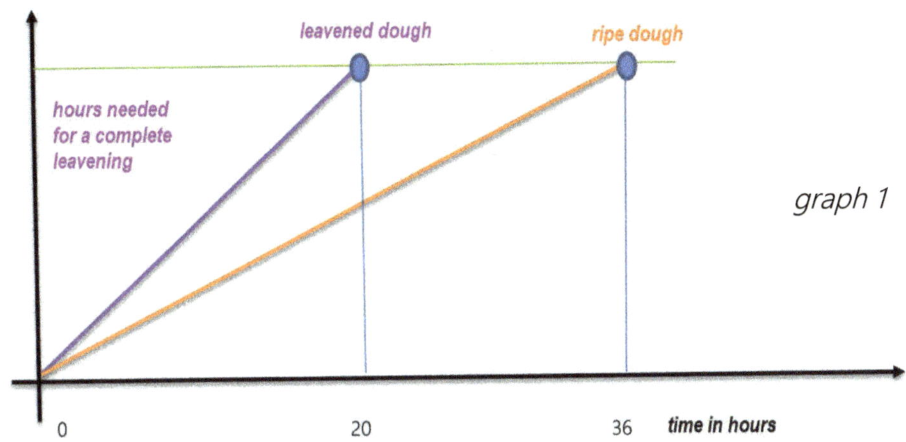

In the first case (graph 1) the fermentation process is in purple, the enzymatic hydrolysis in orange color and it is thought for a maturation of 36 hours suitable for the strength flour used. As we see in this example (graph 1), which concerns fermentation without a refrigerator, leavening reaches its peak after 20 hours, while maturation reaches the top after 36 hours, in short, if we bake after 20 hours we have a leavened pizza but not quite mature.

Second case: leavening supported by chill

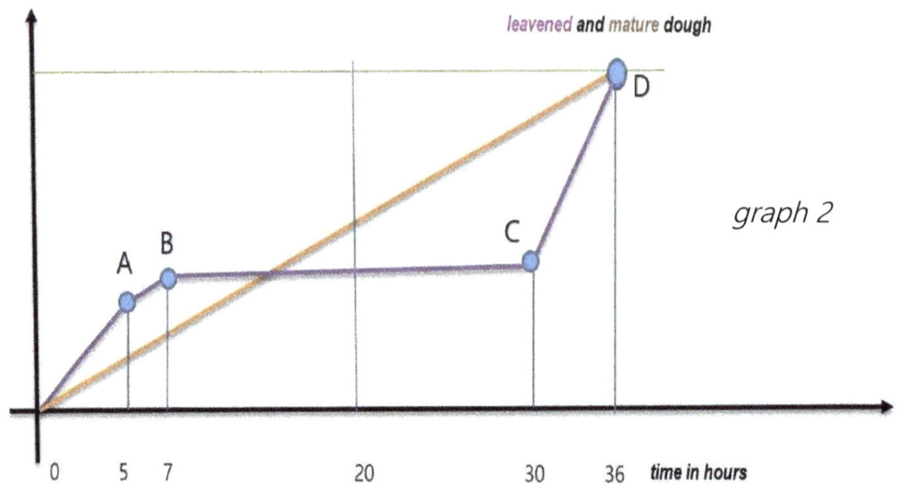

In the second case (graph 2) the dough was placed in the fridge after 5 hours of fermentation (point A). It is observed that the rising (in purple color) will continue slower and slower until it stops at the point B, where the dough will have dropped below 4 °C which will inhibit the yeast (the cooling of the dough pizza dough balls up to the inhibition temperature can last even some hours and depends on the size of the same, their temperature, the quality of the fridge and how many boxes will be inserted). The stretch from A to B matches the time necessary to bring the dough under 4 °C (variable time), the section from B to C highlights the finishing of the growth of the dough following the stop of fermentation, instead the maturation due to enzymes continues (orange line).

After 30 hours (point C), the leavening has been restored by removing the boxes from the refrigerator, you will obtain at the end a leavened and ripe product (point D).

But at this point a question arises, why use a strong flour and opt for a long leavening out of the fridge, if I can use a flour with a lower W, perhaps ancient grains, which will certainly have a shorter leavening but thanks to the help of the refrigerator will that be much more digestible? This is what I meant by the sentence on page12: "A dough made with strong flour that has had a long leavening, it is not necessarily better than a dough made with weak flour, which has had a lower leavening time, but that has matured a lot in the fridge cell".

If our concern is a less strong gluten mesh due to proteolysis, we can partly overcome this difficulty with mass maturation, which we will discuss later and which allows us to deal with lower W flours, we can also add a 0.5% of salt and prefer oxygenation techniques in order to consolidate the gluten mesh.
I do not want to demonize strong flours, without which many products would not be possible, but it is my intention to try to minimize those effects that too often give way to intolerances and indigestible pizzas.

Many of my doughs are made with Biga, which involves high-gluten flour (strong flour), but in these cases, I push the maturation to the maximum and in any case, I use flour with medium or low W in the refreshment, as well as paying close attention to the quality of the raw material. Let us not forget that for high hydrations, we need W from 330 upwards, it is also true that in such cases the enzymatic hydrolysis that gives rise to the maturation processes is very high due to the large quantity of water.

This chapter, in my opinion very important, highlights the great difference that exists between leavening and maturation, for example, I could prepare a dough with medium strength flour, put it in a cell at 3 °C for 36 hours and then let it rise only 4 hours to obtain so a digestible and leavened pizza, while if I did a single fermentation of 18 hours at room temperature, which would include strong flour, I would be far from achieving this result. Having reached this point, we cannot fall into the error of thinking that 18 hours of leavening are better than 4, we must look at the process as a whole. Once the concept of the diversity that exists between leavening and maturation has been clarified, it is time to understand what the behavior of the yeast will be when the leavening is restored.

When you remove the product from the fridge, there will be many sugars available for the yeast and this thanks to the splitting of the starch due to the amylases that have worked undisturbed, it follows that the yeast will have much to feed on and will act faster at the same time , via proteolysis that took place simultaneously, the glutinic mesh will be weaker and less able to retain the CO_2 that will be produced.

Increasing maturation for a long time (72 hours or more) the result will be a lower pizza, the edge will tend to rise less and less this due to the failure of the gluten mesh, which will display micro-holes (or more pronounced porosity) and will not be able to retain carbon dioxide.

The best time to use the dough is generally from 48 to 72 hours, depending on the product you want to make: for example, we will see that a Neapolitan pizza will never have a dough with too long maturation timing, resulting in a low edged pizza; even doughs made with high hydration and a high percentage of Biga or yeast, will not have long maturations or will be difficult to manage (round pizza). In this late event, to get a good maturation, you can opt for mass maturation of the dough in the refrigerator. This is because if the pizza balls are created after all the dough has been taken out of the refrigerator (maturation period), the glutinic mesh is partly rebuilt, this will make it easier to process by hand, and the gases will be better retained inside and a higher edge will be obtained. This is also the reason why the dough for the Neapolitan Pizza is left to rest in a large container and the formation of the pizza dough balls is made 6/8 hours before use, during which time the leavening takes place.

Direct dough: 36-hour mass maturation, W 240 flour, spicy gorgonzola topping, and milk's flower mozzarella, ready to be baked.

Effects on leavening with the cold technique

Till referring to the graphs, in the first case (graph 1), without the use of cold, the dough rises at room temperature for 20 hours.
In the second case (graph 2) instead, we notice that the time in which the dough rises out of the fridge is less than 20 hours, 5 + 2 + 6 = 13 hours (sections from 0 to A, from A to B and from C to D).
A frequent question that was often asked to me during the courses is this: "Why if we put the dough in the fridge, do we have to let it rise less than as if we had to leave it at room temperature?
Proteolysis and amylolysis provide the answer, but let's go step by step.
Still referring to the second case (graph 2), the dough in the initial phase is out of the fridge and behaves exactly as in the first case (graph 1), therefore the first 5 leavening hours are equal. We know that we want to stop the fermentation to let the enzymes work, so we block the fermentation process by putting it "in the cold". At this point, however, proteolysis comes into play, which will begin to weaken the gluten mesh more, as the dough will remain more in the fridge, the amylases meanwhile will have produced a lot of sugar.
Then, when we remove the dough from the fridge, as soon as the fermentation restarts, as the temperature rises, the yeasts will have many more nutrients than at the beginning and will produce CO_2 faster, but the glutinic mesh will be weaker and will not be able to hold back the gases as it could have done at the very beginning. The conclusion is that the same dough will no longer be able to withstand the same fermentation hours (the CO_2 would come out of the micro-holes that proteolysis has created in the gluten mesh) which would instead bear, without the aid of cold.

When we use the cold technique, we must consider that the more we leave the dough in the fridge, the fewer hours it can withstand the fermentation at (RT) (19/21 °C) once removed from the cell.

The cold and its effect on the alveolation of the crumb

The crumb's hole (alveoli) with the cold technique tends to vary because the bubbles of carbon dioxide undergo a change, in particular, they will tend to shrink with the cold, but when the dough enters the oven, it will regain size and will mix with other bubbles giving rise to a more irregular crumb's holes, with large bubbles due to the union of several particles of CO_2.
This is one of the reasons why, if the cold technique is used, it is necessary not to let the product rise too much in the first phase, before blocking its rising. (Giorilli & Lipetskaia, Panificando, 2003)

Let us also remember that a first leavening is essential: if we immediately stop fermentation with the help of the cold we will not be able to obtain a product properly developed once extracted from the refrigerator.

At this point, a thought is needed, when, in the dough, the oxygen has been completely consumed by the multiplication of fungi (yeast), the metabolism of the cells changes and takes the name of fermentation. If any air residue remains in the boxes and if the dough is placed immediately in the cold, rising does not begin and the production of carbon dioxide remains compromised; both because it is not adequately produced (the yeast still has oxygen and fermentation does not start properly) and because of the stiffening of the Gluten mesh that will hinder the formation of alveoli. In this case, the pizza ball will remain small and underdeveloped even after it has been brought back to room temperature.

To sum up, if we use the cold technique we must reduce the initial rising time to a minimum (reducing it to a minimum does not mean eliminating it completely, an error that many make), the dough always requires a period outside the fridge from one to more hours, the time varies depending on the product type, the Biga doses, yeast or temperature.

For example, if I use weak flours, it will reduce the R.T. phase to a minimum, sometimes even just one hour. Last but not least, my first concern is not leavening, but maturation. How many people say "pizza has leavened in my belly", yet this phrase is not reflected in reality since yeasts die at 50 °C and therefore cannot continue to produce CO_2 and ethyl alcohol.

Pizza with zucchini, ricotta, mozzarella on a zucchini and fennel cream. The golden-brown color is synonymous with a long fermentation, which leads to the formation of abundant sugars that contribute to a pronounced Maillard reaction.

DOUGH MATURATION TECHNIQUES

We have understood that order to obtain a good dough and the consequent decomposition of complex or indigestible parts into simpler and easily assimilated parts, maturation is extremely important. We also are more aware that strong flours are a problem, given that some enzymes capable of breaking down certain bonds are lacking.

Having said that, let's try to see some methods to be used to obtain a good maturation:

1. maturation in the fridge after portioning pizza loaves
2. mass maturation in the fridge before portioning dough pizza balls
3. mass maturation at room temperature (RT) without yeast

Maturation in cold storage after portioning pizza balls

The most commonly used and simplest technique at the moment is to make the dough as normal, cut out the dough, make the pizza balls, put them in the pizza dough boxes, start rising at room temperature and then put the pizza boxes in a cold storage at a temperature of 3 °C. At this point, we wait for 24 to 72 hours depending on the strength of the flour used and the hydration is given (strong flour has strong gluten and holds the proteolysis better). If high hydration is used, this accelerates all enzymatic hydrolysis processes, in which case very long refrigeration times are problematic or even not feasible (for the round classic pizza).

Mass maturation in the fridge before portioning pizza dough balls, which will be done the day of use

This is also an excellent technique, it involves the creation of the dough and a resting time of about 15/30 minutes on the workbench, all is then placed in a large container with a lid and put in the fridge at 3 °C for a period of 18/48 hours (you need to give the folds to the dough before placing it in the container). The pizza dough balls must be done the same day of service and there is the possibility of not using all the mass of dough, but only the part you need, while the rest can remain in the refrigerator and continue to rest.

To proceed with the creation of the pizza dough balls, however, you have to wait until the mass removed from the refrigerator reaches a temperature that can work it, around 18 °C. After the formation of the pizza dough balls, the dough is leavened before its final use. At this point, the leavening times vary according to the type of flour used, for example, if you use a flour with low W (240) the leavening at room temperature is unlikely to exceed 4/6 hours, in a case like this the ideal is, therefore, to make the dough balls at 2 or 3 pm if you opt for the evening service.

One of the advantages of this maturation technique is related to the time, in fact, if the dough is made after the evening service, it can be put directly into the container with a lid. After giving it the folds, you let it rest for about 15 minutes and immediately after the container goes into the refrigerator without having to make the pizza dough balls that require a time proportional to their amount. In the evening after the service, we are often tired, this technique is convenient and effective, not only, but if you have little storage space it is the best system.

It is also an excellent method to perform maturation if you make the dough at home. I happen to organize theme nights with friends who have a wood oven, not being equipped with a professional refrigerator where you can insert the pizza dough boxes 60x40, this is the only valid way to have a final product ripe and leavened. I simply put the dough in the fridge and after 36 hours, generally after lunch or in the early afternoon, I make the pizza dough balls that will be ready in the evening.

Please note:
the yeast doses for these working methods are very low. In the winter about 2.5 grams per kg of flour are used, in the summer 1 gram or 1 gram and a half always per kg of flour.

The term mass maturation means a period of time during which the dough is not rising or fermenting (the dough is below 4 °C), so some similar terms such as mass proving or slow proving have a different meaning.

Mass maturation at room temperature (R.T.) without yeast (a re-mix follows)

It is not always possible to use the refrigerator, let's not be afraid, it is still possible to obtain a mature dough, it remains important to have a controlled temperature that is between 19 and 21 °C.

It could be defined as autolysis since no yeast and refrigerator are used, in reality, it is necessary to make a small but significant expedient to prolong this technique of maturation beyond 14/16 hours.

Method

It is kneaded leaving aside 10 or 20% of water, do not put the yeast, but add the salt, the reason we find it in the fact that, since the gliadin is less soluble in salt water, the addition of salt gives rise to greater quantities of short-fiber gluten, this makes the dough more compact, in short, it reinforces gluten. The addition of salt also has an antiseptic effect and determines the true difference between autolysis and this maturation technique.

The dough is then placed in a container with a lid and left at room temperature (R.T.) for 24 hours. After this time we have to put the mass back into the mixer, add the water left aside, the yeast, the oil and proceed with the dough. Once this operation is finished, let it rest for 20 minutes covered, form the pizza dough balls and wait for it to rise. We have thus succeeded in making a dough that will be leavened and mature without the help of the fridge. Care must be taken, for with this technique, a total hydration could be subject to some variations; it is usually advisable to lower it by 2% due to the proteolysis which weakens the gluten mesh unless very strong flours are used.

The dough cannot be left at room temperature (R.T.) for too long without using the fridge. I remember that water and flour left at room temperature are the first steps towards sourdough. Surely with this method, if we spend the 24 hours, we will have a bacterial flora composed also of lactobacilli and since the antagonist "yeast" is not present, the lactobacilli will be totally free to express its nutritional "point of view". An increase in the acidity of the dough will follow, a positive factor that, if combined with the use of small yeast doses for a long leavening, it could give birth to a very interesting product.

It is very important to work in an utterly spick-and-span environment, containers, kneader, counters and everything else, must be spotless.

We have understood that maturation is a goal to which we must aim to arrive at a dough with a capital "D", we just have to choose which method to use. We have no excuses, you can get a more digestible product whether you use professional refrigerators, or your space is limited, or even if you are in an emergency and we do not have a refrigerator available.

This method can also be used with the help of the cold room, some special cases of this maturation apply to those mixtures that need a lot of yeast, such as 2% or 3%, and less strong flours (sheet pan pizza and other products).

Let's not forget that gluten still plays an important role, even if it is not very thick (weak flour), it must be able to give life to a leavened product (developed), otherwise, we will get a compact mass without alveolation. The right combination of flour, maturation, and fermentation is very important.

Maturation and cooking

We must bear in mind that cooking also affects digestibility, since a poorly cooked product certainly does not help digestion, in fact, the starch in particular, if raw is very indigestible. The pizza must be cooked both above and below, it must have a burnished color (Maillard reaction), below it must have small brownish spots (again Maillard reaction), the edge or cornice, once opened, must have a detached alveolation and must not be compact and moist. From a certain point of view, I consider cooking to be the final step of maturation.

*In the picture, I just baked a pizza Margherita
done with the Neapolitan dough.*

*I HAVE DELIBERATELY TREATED MATURATION FIRST IN
ORDER TO UNDERSTAND ITS IMPORTANCE*

*THE MATURATION MUST BE CONSIDERED REGARD-
LESS OF THE TYPE OF DOUGH THAT WE ARE GO-
ING TO MAKE.*

*TO UNDERSTAND HOW TO PUT IT INTO PRACTICE
I REPEAT IT BY COMBINING IT WITH THE TECH-
NIQUES OF DOUGHING*

TO DO SO, LET'S TALK ABOUT PIZZA DOUGHS

Types of pizza Dough used in Italy

There are **three** different **methods** for **mixing** the ingredients

- The Straight Dough Method, or direct method
- The Semi-Directs Dough Method with part of the previous dough
- The Indirect Dough Method with *Biga or Poolish*

The straight **dough method** is the easiest and most widely used in the world.

Overview:

Each dough has different times and methods of preparation that depend on the strength of the flour, hydration and other factors.

A dough with weak flour requires a lower quantity of water and has shorter preparation times, as long as it is not wholemeal or not very refined flours, with cereals, or semolina.

With the same flour, the dough can be divided into very soft, soft and dry, wherewith " very soft" we have percentages of water above 64%, "soft" from 56 to 63%, "dry" below 54%.

The Straight Dough Method, or direct method

All the ingredients are mixed together and in a single phase, water, flour, yeast, fat, and salt.

I advise not to put salt and yeast together, they should not come into immediate contact with each other.

The direct method is the simplest and the most used in the pizzeria sector, unfortunately in many cases short leavening is still used, sometimes even leavening that goes from the afternoon to the same evening. We have seen that a proper maturation must be considered between 24 and 36/48 hours.

The direct dough allows the use of weak flours, which is generally not possible with the indirect method.

How to proceed to prepare a direct dough:

- *the flour is poured into the kneading machine, then the yeast is crumbled, about 80% of water is poured and the machine is started, oil is put on and the remaining water is poured. After 5 minutes from the beginning of the processing, salt is added.*

The duration of the processing depends on the strength of the flour and hydration, times can vary substantially, you must learn to recognize when you get to the dough ready or at that time when the dough is smooth, with good surface tension and detached from the mixer.

Each dough needs a short period of rest on the work-bench covered with film. The wet canvas is often not in compliance with local regulations.

Here's a dough that can be considered ready, is well strung, it is smooth and detached from the walls, not sticky to the touch.
It is a good idea, after this moment, to wait a few minutes and give a few more turns with the mixer before putting it on the counter and work it.

I kneaded the dough and placed it on the bench, now it must be covered with film and left to rest.

During the initial resting phase, the starch granules absorb liquids better, and in this period the structure of the newly formed gluten tends to stabilize.

The correct realization of dough also lies in observing these details.

Up to this point, all the direct mixtures are practically the same, from here it is necessary to decide how to proceed, thus choosing the maturation technique to be used.

1. Direct dough method at room temperature (R.T.) without using the fridge
(without maturation)

After making the dough, proceed to weigh the pizza dough balls, which will be placed in pizza dough boxes, then wait for the fermentation and then use it. I never use this method of working since it does not lead to obtaining a product that satisfies the rules of digestibility I mentioned in this book.

2. Direct dough method with cold technique *(maturation of pizza dough balls in a cold room).*

After the dough, we proceed to the preparation of the pizza dough balls which will be placed in pizza boxes, we will have the first leavening at room temperature (R.T.) for a period varying from a minimum of 1 hour up to 2 or 3 hours, subsequently, the boxes will be placed in the cold store at 3 °C for 24/36/72 hours. Before use, fermentation is completed until the product has reached the R.T.

3. Direct dough method with mass rest and cold technique *(no pizza dough balls are prepared in this first phase).*

Place the mass of the dough, giving folds, inside a container with a lid, let it rest for about 10 minutes at room temperature (R.T.) then place everything in the cold store at 3 °C. After the time set for the maturation, which will vary from about 24 to 48 hours, the pizza dough balls will be made and then they will have to leaven at room temperature (R.T.) as I wrote in the maturation chapter.

4. Direct dough method with mass resting at R.T. (mass maturation at R.T. dough without yeast and oil but with salt).

During the kneading phase, leave about 20% of the water apart, add the salt provided, do not put the yeast and oil. The mass of the dough is placed in a container with a lid and left to rest at room temperature (R.T.) for 24 hours. After this period, put everything back in the mixer, adding the water left aside with the yeast dissolved in it and proceed with the remixing, inserting the oil after about a minute or two. At the end of the process, let it rest for about 15 minutes and proceed to the cutting of the pizza dough balls, which will only have to leavened at this point. *The addition of salt has an antiseptic effect by stopping unwanted microorganisms as well as making the glutinic mesh stronger.*

5. Direct dough method with Autolysis.

Autolysis is a good processing technique, it was developed by the French bakery expert Raymond Calvel, who noticed that, when the dough has the opportunity to be composed initially only of water and flour, without other additions, it comes out significantly improved in the final part. Calvel has conducted a series of studies on this subject that have confirmed his theory. The process of autolysis is however very simple for us Pizzaioli to carry out and takes place in three phases:

1. Only flour and water are mixed. 2. Let the mass rest at R.T. for a certain period. 3. We proceed to re-mix the mass, adding what was previously excluded, salt, yeast, oil (if provided). Once the dough is finished, make the pizza dough balls, which can then be placed again in the fridge to continue ripening or to be used after rising. There are different schools of thought on the duration of autolysis, I opt for a time frame that varies from 6 to 12 hours and uses 100% of the flour and 80% of the expected water.

With this technique and autolysis times from 12 hours upwards, it is advisable to reduce the hydration of the dough by about 2 percentage points due to proteolysis that weakening the gluten mesh.

You will have noticed that points 4 and 5 of this paragraph are very similar, but there is a substantial difference, which consists of the addition of salt and the timing. Autolysis does not provide for salt and the times cannot, therefore, last more than 12 hours or little more, in the method used at point 4 instead we have an accentuated maturation of at least 24 hours and here is the reason for the salt.

Dough with Biga and flour with cereal mix.
In such mixtures, it is important to make pizza dough balls at least 230 grams or it will be difficult to shape the pizza disc.
Flours that have bran parts tend to raise the P/L value of the dough which becomes easy to break during processing, in addition, the bran parts or the cereals, create breakpoints by spreading the pizza ball.

Semi-direct dough method

All the ingredients are kneaded in the direct mix at the same time, but a portion of a previously prepared dough is added, which has already matured a period of fermentation.
This piece of old dough is previously stored in a closed container, slightly larger than the size of the portion of the dough itself.
It is added in different sizes ranging from 10% to 25%, with an optimal dose of around 20%. Depending on the percentage added, the dose of fresh yeast to be added varies, indicatively from 0.1 to 0.3%, depending on the product to be obtained. All the maturation techniques described above are valid.

Indirect dough method: Biga and Poolish

In the first phase, a pre-ferment is prepared with flour, water and yeast, this pre-ferment is let leaven for the established time. In a second phase, the ingredients used to finish the dough are added, flour, water, salt, oil, malt.

*In the picture we see a series of pizzas freshly baked
and ready to be served at the tables.*

BIGA dry pre-ferment

The realization of Biga, that is our pre-ferment, is not difficult, what is more complicated is to understand the exact dose of refreshment in proportion to the type of dough you want to get. We have to see Biga as the yeast, which, however, due to its size, also brings water and additional flour to the final dough. If we think in these terms, we can understand some crucial aspects.

Biga doses preparation: 44% of water and 1% fresh yeast.

When we prepare the Biga we use only water, flour, and fresh yeast, we knead for a few minutes, we don't have to obtain a smooth glutinic mesh, the preferment must remain raw and lumpy, but without free flour, generally it is kneaded at minimum speed in the kneading machine for two minutes and then in reverse for 2 or 3 minutes. If you do not have the reverse gear in the mixer you work from 4 to 6 minutes at a minimum speed depending on the dose to be prepared. However, the Biga in small quantities is often prepared by hand.
Kneading machines are usually used on a low-speed-mode to prevent the dough to be worked excessively and also to prevent it from heating.
The Biga should not be kneaded even too little, in order not to leave free flour yet to be incorporated into the dough.
The container must be able to contain about twice the Biga dough.
The container must allow an upward thrust and not lateral, so it is recommended to use a narrow container rather than a large and low tank.
A container that encloses the dough, allows a better and faster fermentation than a large container with low sides, this is mainly because of the different temperature that develops inside the dough. Let's not forget that the Biga must ferment and not leaven, even if a minimum of leavening always takes place. To avoid using film on the container each time to start the fermentation, I recommend to get a

container with a hermetic lid, possibly transparent, ideally, it would have to be different and in various sizes, allowing you to prepare different doses of pre-ferment, depending on the different amount of work between holidays and weekdays, which provides a less product preparation. You may wonder why a container for a 4kg Biga is not good for a 1kg Biga, the answer is found in the following paragraph.

Biga unfermented or badly made

If, after fermentation, a Biga has incrustations or a dark brown color, then oxidized parts, generally, it has either been mixed too little (there is free flour) and has not correctly absorbed the necessary water, or it has been placed in a too-large container and then oxidized because of the excessive quantity of air with which it has come into contact. A Biga with these characteristics allows the growth of Saccharomyces Cerevisiae, intended as multiplication, but it does not have correct alcoholic fermentation and creates the conditions for the multiplication of unwanted microorganisms that interfere with the yeasts, moreover, the pH of the preferment dough will be higher.

The flour to be used for Biga

The pre-ferment Biga needs strong flours (W from 340/350), in the refreshment, you can combine flours of lower strength.

How to calculate the refreshment *(what to add at the preferment)* to be used based on the amount of Biga

Let's start with that concept:
In terms point of view, we indicate the weight of dough, referring to the weight of flour, that is, if I say that I make a dough of 10 kg I mean that to obtain it, I will use 10 kg of flour, in the same way, if I say "Biga of 1 kg" I mean to make it, I will use 1 kg of flour.

If I used 1 kg of Biga, it would have been made up of 1 kg of flour, plus the water used to prepare it. In the case of 44% of water, 1 kg of Biga will weigh 1.44 kg (I have neglected the 10 grams of yeast used for fermentation).

We must, therefore, refer to the following "formula":

$$Total\ dough\ =\ Biga\ +\ Refreshment$$

All becomes clear with this example:

Let's suppose that I want to make a total dough that uses 10 kg of flour and in which there is 25% of Biga (Biga hydrated to 44%). At the same time, I want the total dough to be 56% hydrated, so I will have to adjust as follows:

- Total flour: 10 Kg.
- Total water: 5,6 Litres (56% of 10 Kg)

of which
- Biga flour: 2,5 Kg (25% of 10 kg)
- Water used in Biga: 1.1 Litres (44% of 2.5 Kg)

Here's our refreshment

$$flour\ refreshment\ 7.5\ kg\ =\ 10\ kg - 2.5\ kg$$
$$water\ refreshment\ 4.5\ litres\ =\ 5.6\ litres - 1.1\ litres$$

We calculate the salt, oil, and malt according to the percentages we intend to use on the total weight of the flour and, in the case of the previous example, on the ten kg of the total dough.

Biga fermentation temperature

The fermentation temperature for the Biga should be between 18 and 20 °C."

I'd like to clarify an important point

I have used the term pre-ferment for indirect doughs, but this is only to avoid confusing the existing terminology on the web. The actual correct term is pre-mixture or better, pre-dough, because both Biga and Poolish ferment just like any flour mixed with water. It does not make sense to me to use the term pre-ferment, since it implies that something is fermented before it actually ferments. In my books in Italian, I have always used the term pre-mixture for this reason.

Poolish, unlike Biga, is a liquid preferment.
It has a flour-water ratio of 1 to 1 and the doses of yeast used vary according to the hours of fermentation of the same.

Poolish is more acidic than Biga, it also offers a different result in terms of alveolation, which is generally more compact and uniform.
The management and preparation are in my opinion simpler than the Biga and the final dough is more manageable thanks to the lower thrust (less leavening power when used at the same doses as Biga).
Being a very liquid dough, it is almost always prepared by hand directly into the container which will then be covered during fermentation. Why do you say by hand? Well, if we prepare it in the mixer then it becomes problematic, if not impossible, to remove it, since it is liquid and the tank is fixed.

The doses of fresh yeast to be used in Poolish

The following table shows the indicative values on the quantity of fresh yeast to be used in Poolish according to the hours of fermentation of the same, we note immediately that unlike Biga a Poolish can also have a very short path. My opinion about this is that it makes little sense to use a pre-ferment without a fermentation such as to return a whole series of characteristics, personally, I do not use this pre-ferment before the 12/14 hours of rising.

Poolish fermentation hours	Doses of fresh yeast in grams
2	2,5%
4-5	1,5%
7-8	0,5%
10-12	0,2%
16-18	0,1%

Flour to be used in Poolish

Medium strength flours can also be used, but as Poolish is more suitable for soft dough it is good to consider this factor in the making phase.

When is the Poolish ready to be used

Many say it has to double, others triple. A good signal comes from the surface, which must have numerous bubbles, and is ready when the surface starts to become concave or, as they say in slang when it starts "to sag".

Refreshment with Poolish and doses to be used

Poolish, unlike Biga, is used in smaller doses, 20% is, in my opinion, a very good percentage, given the strong flavors it brings, but you can get up to 30%.
The alveolation of the final dough compared to Biga is different, it is generally more uniform in size, with less pronounced alveoli, Poolish releases a particular taste that must please, also pushes less than Biga and more gradually, this is the reason for the different alveolation.

Poolish fermentation temperature

Poolish fermentation temperature should be between 20 and 22 °C.

Indirect dough method (Biga and Poolish), how to make the maturation of the dough.

If we think of Biga and Poolish exactly as they were a piece of yeast, we immediately understand that the maturation is performed as already seen for direct doughs and we will put it into practice after refreshment with the two following methods:

1. Maturation of pizza dough balls in the fridge.
We proceed to the preparation of pizza dough balls that will be placed in pizza dough boxes. First leavening in R.T. for a variable time of at least one hour until 2 or 3 hours, then the dough is placed in a cold room at 3°C.
For this method a clarification is needed: if the dose of Biga is high, for example, 40% or more and if the Poolish is short fermentation, then with high doses of yeast, the dough will be placed in the refrigerator almost immediately or it will be difficult to stop the leavening, this happens because of the strong push generated by the pre-leavened (Biga or Poolish).

2. Mass maturation without preparation of the pizza balls.
Place the mass of the dough, giving folds, inside a container with a lid, let it rest for about 10 minutes at R.T. then place everything in the cold room at 3°C. After the time set for the maturation, which will vary from about 24 to 48 hours, the dough pizza loaves will be made, which will then have to leavened to R.T.

Conclusions

Choosing the method of mixing has a lot of influence on the final product, however, it must be combined with the maturation techniques. Kneading and using the product without maturation is never a good choice, especially if the flours used are strong.

The advantages of the indirect dough method

These advantages consist of a more lasting conservation (better shelf-life), a much more intense scent, profound taste, large and more developed alveoli, and high digestibility. The majority of the acidity obtained in the pre-ferment dough (Biga or Poolish) with lactic fermentation (development of lactic acid) implies a better and more lasting protection from germs and other kinds of contaminations, an odour development caused by the creation of amino acids transformed into aromatic substances during the cooking and the splitting in simple molecules that are more easily digestible from the organism due to the fermentation process being completed.

The disadvantages of the indirect dough method:

The disadvantages are the difficult management of the final dough.

Pizza with finely chopped zucchini cooked on a basis of milk's flower mozzarella, sweet gorgonzola, and truffle oil. The dough is direct, made with flour W 220
maturation is 36 hours, fermentation is 5 hours at R.T.

The management of the dough in the fridge

When we put the dough in the refrigerator we have a technical time before it falls below 4 °C, this time varies from the number of boxes that we put in but especially varies between the boxes placed at the top near the fan and the lower ones. In a situation like the one in the photo, the upper boxes will cool down quickly, while the central and lower ones may take several hours, it becomes important to invert them after the first hour.

Do not underestimate this aspect or you will find yourself faced with a leavened dough part and another completely still. Adding a shelf in the fridge makes it easier to reverse the boxes and the final management.

For the doses of Biga and Poolish to use in the
dough, see the chapter on yeast on page 93.

THE RIGHT TEMPERATURE OF A DOUGH

Temperature plays a very important role in the reproduction of yeasts. We know that the excellent reproductive is between 25°C and 30°C, the excellent fermentative also reaches 35°C.

Having said that, it is clear enough that dough must come out of the mixer at a certain temperature, but how do we decide this temperature?

First of all, let's see at what temperature the dough should come out:

Hydration	Optimum dough temperature
Dry or hydrated doughs with up to 53% hydration	temperature 22/23 °C
Soft or hydrated doughs from 54 to 56%.	temperature 23 °C
Soft or hydrated doughs from 57% to 70%	temperature 23/25 °C

Factors that influence the temperature of the dough during preparation:

- *flour temperature*   *(F.T.)*
- *water temperature*   *(H_2O. T.)*
- *room temperature*   *(R.T.)*
- *the temperature generated by the mixer due to friction* **(M.T.)**

To obtain a dough at the ideal temperature, the water temperature must vary, which is generally the only element on which we can intervene. This is why the formulas for calculating the temperature of the dough are also identified as formulas for calculating the water temperature.

It is usually assumed that the temperature of the flour is one degree lower than the room temperature.

Be careful, however, because if you live in tropical places the flour is stored in cells or simply in the refrigerator, which could be done by us in summer, but in that case, we must remember to measure the temperature of the flour and insert it in the formula, will not be worth the value of one degree less than room temperature. My advice is to always measure the temperature with a thermometer since some storage areas are located in different places than those in which we knead.

Dough temperature formula

$$H_2O.T. = (desired\ dough\ temperature \times 3) - (F.T. + R.T. + M.T.)$$

The kneading machines cause a heating of the dough that varies depending on whether it is a kneading machine with twin arms, spiral or fork. The table below shows the reference grades for the type of kneading machine used. I report the table as it is known in the bakery and pizzeria environment, but I recommend to carry out checks with a thermometer and some experiments since I personally found different values depending on the brand of mixer used.

Dough mixers such as ovens are not all the same, for the same type, not all provide equal heating in the processing phase.

Mixer type	M.T. or mixer temperature in °C that the mixer generates on a direct dough at a lower speed
Fork mixers	3 °C
Twin arm mixer (called also double-arm, or diving arm mixer)	6 °C
Spiral mixer	9 °C
Handmade dough	2 °C

The indirect doughs made with the Biga cause greater heating by the mixer due to their hardness. There are those who provide these values for the temperature generated by the various mixers in the case of indirect mixtures in tables, but I prefer not to bring them back because of the variables, in fact, if I use a dose of Biga of 20% it will not be like using a dose of Biga by 60%, so I can hardly say how much friction has increased in general.

For the Biga and the Poolish, a double temperature calculation is used, one relating to the preferment and one to the refreshment.

Dough of my realization with 30% Biga, we can see the strong boost of leavening.
The Biga gives rise to a superior category product.
The dough in question uses 0 W320 flour for the Biga and 0 W260 flour in the refreshment.
I continue with my method of work that involves flour of medium or low strength in the final dough, opting for a long maturation in refrigerators or at controlled temperatures.

Calculation of the water temperature in Biga preparation

The final temperature for a Biga at the end of the mixing must be between 20 and 21 °C. To obtain this result we work, as seen, on the water temperature, the only element that allows us to manage the final temperature.

In the calculation, to know at what temperature the water should be used in our Biga preferment, we start from a fixed number: **55**, to this number, the room temperature **(R.T.)** and the temperature of the flour **(F.T)** are subtracted.

We will then have to calculate the water temperature for the final dough(refreshments), which we know how to obtain by using the general formula.

$$H_2O.T. = (desired\ dough\ temperature \times 3) - (F.T. + R.T. + M.T.)$$

Calculation of the water temperature in Poolish preparation

The Poolish, unlike the Biga, is ready at a higher temperature, therefore, it needs almost lukewarm water. For the calculation of the dough temperature, the formula provides a fixed value of 70, where 70 indicates the ideal sum given by the room temperature combined with that of the flour and water. To this fixed number, the sum of the room temperature and that of the flour is subtracted as follows:

For example, if the room temperature at which you work is 21.5°C and the flour temperature is 20.5°C, then the optimal water temperature is calculated in this way:

$$70 - (21.5 + 20{,}5) = 28\ C°$$

Obviously, even with Poolish, the final dough temperature must be calculated using the general formula.

$$H_2O.T. = (desired\ dough\ temperature \times 3) - (F.T. + R.T. + M.T.)$$

The values of temperature generated by the mixer **(M.T.)** are provided in the table on page 52.

DOUGH FORMATION AND PROCESSING METHODS

What may seems a simple thing is a critical phase in the production process: if the dough is not well done, it is impossible to obtain a good product. In the pizzeria, doughs must be able to be processed manually when we have to shape the pizza. We must not forget that in the pizzeria the manual part is fundamental.
Pizza is like an " espresso" product which must be prepared on the moment.

The primary purpose is therefore to obtain a homogeneous mixture that maintains the desired technological characteristics in order to be subsequently processed, it is, therefore, necessary that all the ingredients are well incorporated and blended in the dough.

We will see that for very hydrated doughs we will have to resort to special processing techniques or we will risk their collapse, having a lot of loose water not able to amalgamate with the flour, with consequent "mush" in the mixer.

We know that the technological properties of a flour determine its behavior in bread-making processes, the quality of the dough and, consequently, the quality of the finished product depends on the technological characteristics.

We also learned that the strength of the flour is the ability to absorb water during the dough and keep carbon dioxide during leavening. I remind you that when the flour is strong to produce a dough with a soft consistency it absorbs a large percentage of water, this mixture is dry, elastic and not sticky, it is a dough that bears long fermentation and gives life to finished products with large alveoli (large crumb's hole) and well developed.

Dough formation: chemical-physical processes

In any kind of dough, regardless of its method of preparation, physical-mechanical, colloidal, biochemical and microbiological processes take place.

A series of chemical-physical processes are initiated in the formation of the dough:

- *starch hydration*
- *interaction between proteins and gluten formation through the mechanical energy of the kneading divided into phases, defined by the resistance of the same, which varies from hard to soft.*
- *incorporation of air providing oxygen for yeasts and promoting oxidation with the formation of groups -S-S- of proteins*
- *formation of saline bonds between amino acid residues*
- *ionic bonds between protein residues due to the presence of NaCl*
- *interaction with lipids and formation of lipoprotein complexes*

Part of these processes is due to the water which:

- *swells starch granules*
- *causes the dissolution of salt*
- *activates enzymatic reactions (starch and protein hydrolysis)*
- *allows nutrient transport*
- *are the indispensable means for the life of the yeast*

The formation of the pizza dough ball is part of the production process and is important. It must be compact, smooth and push upwards.

Effects of dough hydration

The percentage of hydration of the dough plays a very important role, given that it changes the chemical-physical processes.
A greater quantity of water corresponds to a greater swelling of starch, of proteins, to an accentuated action of the protease with relative transformation into peptides, greater global enzymatic activity, a faster transformation of sugars which are nourishment for yeasts and LAB, is obtained also a more marked production of lactic acid, a faster lowering of the pH and a more immediate fermentation.

Hydration is extremely important but based on the product you want to make, each hydration must match an adequate flour.

High hydrations are practicable with strong flours, but I assure you that I have used the same doses of water for flours with identical W and I have obtained different products, this indicates that the behavior of flours, even if they have similar technical datasheets, is not the same and here comes into play practice and our inspiration. Sometimes the dough succeeds well, but then by working it, you realize the differences. Without making all the steps, ranging from kneading to shaping to baking, we cannot realize how it came out the product.

The flour should be carefully selected according to the hours of leavening and maturation that you want to obtain and the type of hydration to which we intend to submit it, it is concerning this principle that I can give the following guidelines:

Types of dough, relative hydration, and speed of the mixer

Dough for traditional pizza	53/56% hydration	The 1-speed mixer is enough
Dough for Neapolitan pizza	60/65% hydration	1 or 2 speed mixer
Dough for sheet pan pizza	58/65% hydration	1 or 2 speed mixer
Dough for pizza peel roman style	78/85% hydration	2-speed mixer needed

As you can see, if the hydration rises, it is important to adjust the speed of the mixer, without a good "machine", which also has a second suitable speed, it is not possible to make dough with high hydration. I have carried out tests with mixtures that reach 100% hydration: with these products, you need a lot of practice and experience, an excellent kneading machine it becomes essential for processing, how is very implement the right rest, which often takes place in the fridge and lasts 8 or 12 or 18 hours.

Hydration also changes according to the grain size of the flour used. Wholemeal flour, re-milled semolina, soya flour, cereal flour, and other coarse flour, absorb up to 6% or 12% than very refined flour. This aspect must be taken into account when using flour mixtures, but it must also be considered that these flours make gluten of inferior quality.

Doughs with a mix of flours that require different hydrations

Let's start from a concept: semolina, wholemeal flours, cereals, or at least less refined, have a higher absorption of water, as well as slower (we know that bran parts have this prerogative, as well as durum wheat flour). As an indication, I could say that these products need from 6% to 12% more water than a very refined flour like the Italian 00. In other words, if for a dough with a 00 I use hydration of 55% and I wanted the same result to the touch with a wholemeal, the latter should be hydrated to about 62%. The same applies to semolina and less refined flours.

Be careful, even the wholemeal flours on the market are not all the same, some have 14% protein and 12%, the same applies to those with a mix of cereals or semolina.

Doughs with low refined flours need more hydration, the formation of heavier loaves and autolysis or a stop-&-go technique.
The choice of raw material is fundamental, but it is necessary to use the right pro-cessing technique.
Raw flours give back strong and particular flavors that make the best of them if pro-cessed as focaccia and stuffed at the end of cooking.

How to calculate the correct hydration of a flour mix

First of all, we need to know how much absorption the less refined flour used in the mix needs.

I am using an example to propose a suitable method for calculating the hydration required in a mix of flours with different water absorption.

Let's suppose we want to prepare a total dough of 5.5 kg of flour, of which 5 kg will be refined flour and 0.5 kg will be wholemeal flour.

We decide we want a dough hydrated to 55%.

If we calculate 55% of the total we will certainly not get the desired consistency, this is because of the greater absorption of water of wholemeal flour compared to refined flour. Let's assume that the wholemeal gives us a consistency similar to the hydration of 55% on the refined flour, with 63% of water, let's see how to proceed in the total calculation of water required for a mixture of this type:

very simply the hydrations necessary for each quantity of flour are broken down and added together.

With the following table I will clear up the concept:

Dough	Hydration	Water needed
5000 refined flour	55%	2750 gr
500 gr wholemeal flour	63%	315 gr
Total 5500 (sum of flour)		3065 gr (sum hydration)

Usually, if we want to mix different flours, we start by establishing the desired hydration as if we were thinking only about the most refined flour used, after which we will add the water required by the flour or semolina that makes up the mix and that needs more hydration.

Wholemeal flour, durum wheat, multi cereal, need more hydration to restore a dough of the same consistency as a dough made with very refined flour.
When we make dough with different flours kind, we must take into account the greater absorption that these flours require.

Stop & go or machine stop with semolina, wholemeal or less refined flours

When we add less refined flours, we know that they absorb more water, **but they also absorb it more slowly**, which could create problems in the kneading phase, since we would not be able to obtain a homogeneous glutinic mesh.
In this type of cases, to obtain a quality product, the less refined flour is first placed in the mixer's bowl, hydrating it with about 50% of the total water and with no less than the water, such as the flour requires; the mixer is activated for 1 or 2 minutes in order to make everything homogeneous and the machine stops, thus allowing the liquids to be gradually absorbed. The stoppage generally lasts around 20 to 30 minutes, after this interval, you add what is missing to finish the dough and to completing the process (the finest flour, yeast, water, oil, and salt after a few minutes).

This system also allows lowering the P/L of less refined flours, as well as improving their amylase activity.

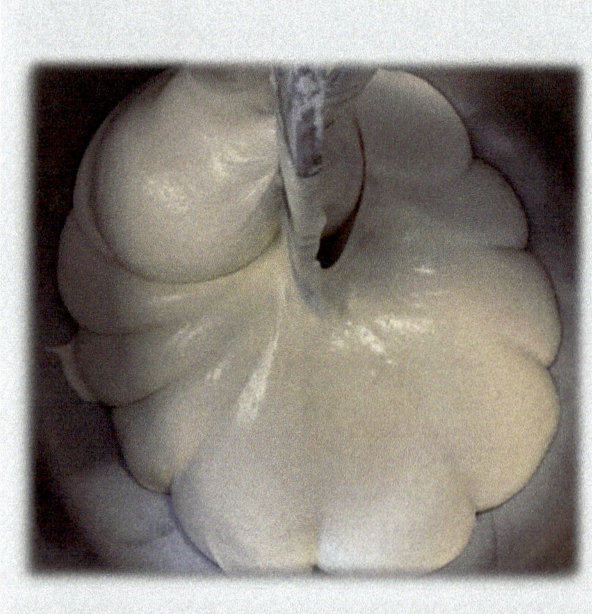

In the picture, one of my dough, with 85% hydration suitable for pizza peel Roman style.
At this point in time, I put the dough in a container after giving it some folds, followed by a period of rest in cold storage for 18 hours, after which I weigh 700 grams loaves that I put to leaven for about 6 hours and, at any rate, until they are almost tripled in volume.

Dough processing

For a traditional dough, the important is to mix the ingredients perfectly, proceeding by
pouring flour, yeast, water and after a few turns of the mixer, the oil, while the salt shall be blended after about 5 or 6 minutes. The dough must be smooth and completely detached from the walls of the bowl, which must be clean. In principle, a weak flour (220/240W) does not withstand processing times of more than 12/14 minutes, a Manitoba flour (350/400 W) can reach 20 minutes and much more.

Dough processing with high hydration

To moisturize a flour with 80% water it must be very strong, even then, however, if you try to pour all the water at once it certainly could not amalgamate, you cannot give life to the glutinic mesh, and you are faced with a broth that does not take shape, the flour cannot absorb the water and the dough "collapses", we have loose water.
In these situations you have to proceed step by step, you start at speed one and, first of all, you have to develop well the glutinic mesh, to achieve this result you have to incorporate a maximum of 65% of water (65% hydration and not 65% of total water to be used in the dough). Once the glutinic mesh has been created, it is continued by slowly pouring the remaining water, being very careful not to let the mixture collapse and passing at a speed of two until a developed mixture is obtained, i.e. smooth and detached from the walls of the mixer's bowl, at this point you can add salt.
Often it is better to work with stop & go machines in order to allow the flour to absorb the water in the best possible way, especially if you want to reach 100% hydration (limit case).
For very hydrated doughs it is essential, for final processing, to give the dough a rest time, which can occur both in the fridge and at room temperatures, in both cases, the dough is reinforced with folds and put into a closed container with a lid. Personally, I prefer to leave it in the refrigerator for about 18 or 24 hours to obtain even a good maturation.
If the resting period is carried out in a dough box container at room temperature, then proceed differently: you give some folds to the dough and place it in the container that will be closed with a lid, after which you wait for the mass to double. At this point, the dough is extracted and the pizza loaves are formed.

Effects of dough oxygenation

In addition to water, the oxygenation of the dough is also extremely important. Oxygen is necessary for the multiplication of yeast cells, not only that, but oxygenation has an effect on proteins and therefore on the glutinic mesh that is reinforced.

With the mechanical action of kneading there is the incorporation of small air bubbles that lose oxygen due to the metabolism of yeasts and due to oxidation phenomena, but there is also the retention of nitrogen gas bubbles in the gluten matrix.

At the end of the mixing, only the nitrogen is trapped, which will constitute the nucleus in which the carbon dioxide produced during fermentation will then be conveyed (Campbell, 2003).

Oxygenation is sometimes accentuated thanks to folds that we will carry out manually once the mass has been extracted from the mixer and placed on the workbench before resting.

Oxygenation restores softness to the dough.

The mixers have great importance in this phase and they manage to make the difference, for example, a twin arms mixer has the advantage of providing greater oxygenation to the dough than a spiral one.

Pizza with fresh zucchini cream, shallots, mint, milk's flower mozzarella, and cherry tomatoes, ready to be baked.

How to insert the ingredients into the kneading machine

Beyond the schools of thought, scientific evidence remains; in short: it is the flour that absorbs water and not the other way around. Doses must be calculated on the flour and not on the water. Many scientific studies have been carried out on this, especially related to the change in the spatial conformation of protein structures. We talk about water absorption and not the other way around: it is not water that absorbs macromolecules.

Throwing the flour into the water tends to make lumps due to the orientation of the polar part.

It then starts from the flour, then crumbles the fresh yeast and starts absorbing the water (not more than 80%), the oil (see the chapter of oil on page 99), after a few minutes (5 or 6) proceed by inserting the salt and continuing with the water until it reaches the homogeneity of the dough, which must be smooth, not sticky and detached from the walls. If malt was used to make the dough, it had to be placed with flour.

Learn to recognize the dough

Each dough takes a different shape in the mixer when it is kneaded, this is mainly due to the amount of water used to make it.

With the same flour, the dough can be divided into hard (or dry), soft, very soft, where with very soft we have percentages of water over 65%, "soft" about 56%, "dry" about 53%.

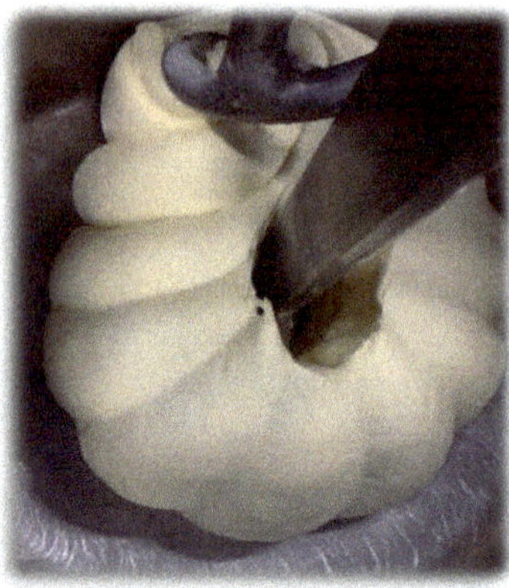 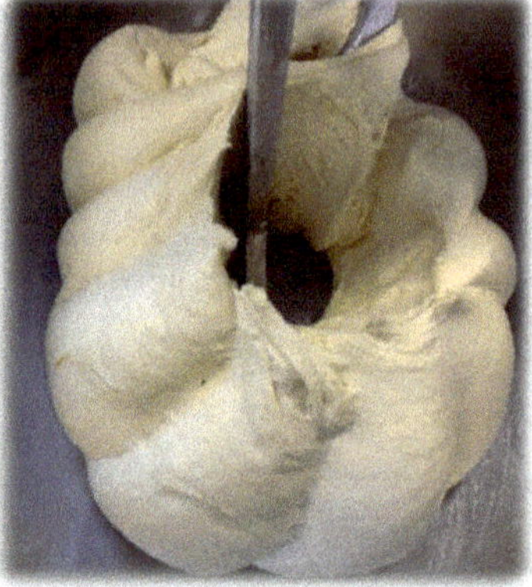 

Above we have a dough that I would define as soft for its 57% hydration, let's not forget its appearance, completely detached from the sidewalls and the base, you can see the typical "ball" closure that detaches it from the bottom. It is smooth, it is not broken and it is certainly ready.

Above we have a dough that I would define as dry or hard for its 53% hydration, its appearance tells us that we are dealing with a dry dough, we notice the big hole in the center near the dough splitter, typical of these mixtures, you can see how it struggles to mix and leaves several wrinkles, the dough mixer is perfectly clean but the dough is not ready. If you continue to knead, you risk overheating it, so you have to fold the dough and let it rest covered on the workbench.

Here instead we have a typical soft dough, always made by myself, which reaches a moisture content of 85% as soon as I turned off the kneading machine it has rightly lowered, but it is detached from the sidewalls and underneath. It is ready, so you give some folds before putting it back in the container for the first phase of rest. If it is left at room temperature it must double before being used, if it is placed in the fridge at 3°C it must remain there at least 18 hours.

The Dough Mixer

We know that a bad dough does not generate a good product, it is fair to say that the kneading is a critical phase.

The fundamental characteristics of the kneading process are

- obtaining a homogeneous and perfectly blended mixture
- obtaining a properly oxygenated mixture that allows the growth of yeasts
- imparting adequate mechanical strength, which is essential for the formation of gluten
- not to overheat the dough

There are mixtures made at low speed and high speed, these two characteristics are binding for the choice of the mixer to be used.

Generally, a good pizza dough mixer has the following characteristics

- homogeneously amalgamates the ingredients
- adequately oxygenates the dough
- does not overheat the dough
- has second speed
- has reverse gear

Not all mixers are the same, on the contrary, some are exceptional, others are barely sufficient for the purpose, some are even not suitable.
The dough mixers used in bread-making are generally much more complex and expensive than those used in pizzerias.

The most common mixers used in bread-making and pizzeria:

- fork mixer
- twin arm mixer or double arms or diving arm
- spiral mixer

Fork mixers, suitable for hard doughs even with only 35% hydration, allow better development of gluten and dough, they generate a limited increase in temperature and are the most widespread in France.
Twin arms mixers are used for medium-hard and soft doughs from 45% to 80% hydration, they simulate manual work, oxygenate the dough very well and increase relatively the temperature of the dough.
Spiral mixers are for various types of dough from 45% to 85% hydration, are the most used in pizzerias even though they have the inconvenience of the fixed bowl so they are not very suitable for large piers of work. The best ones have double speed, reverse gear and possibility to set work programs. There are various brands of this type since they are very simple, but only some companies offer an excellent product and can return well mixed and oxygenated doughs.

Each mixer increases the temperature of the dough in a different way

Mixer kind	M.T. or mixer temperature in °C that the mixer generates on a direct dough at a lower speed
Fork mixer	3 °C
Twin arms mixer	6 °C
Spiral mixer	9 °C
Manual kneading	2 °C

Despite the table, be sure to check always with a thermometer the degree of heating generated by the mixer you use.

Choosing the dough mixer

After the oven, the dough mixer or dough kneading machine is the most important element. With a kneading machine too small we are forced to divide the doughs drastically, lengthening the working time, but if it is oversized we will have problems with too small doughs.

A two-speed, high-quality machine is always the right choice so that we can work with high hydration levels.

On the speed, I could open a whole chapter, since they vary a lot from model to model, for example, some are one speed at 120 RPM and others are one speed, at 90 RPM others at 110 RPM. As for the second speed, which not all do not have, it should be at least 180 RPM; if you want to work with very hydrated dough, the best would be a 220 RPM. We know that a dry dough or a Biga must be processed slowly, while soft dough needs more speed, not to mention high-hydration products for which speed is essential.

MALT in the dough

Pearl Barley

Malt is a product of vegetable origin, specifically a derivative of cereals

The term "malt" generally refers to barley, but it can also be produced from other types of cereals, such as wheat, rice, rye, sesame, corn, and others.
The common characteristic of all types of malt is the presence of maltose disaccharide, which is obtained thanks to the hydrolytic action of the amylases that have separated the starch of origin, in more understandable words, the malt slowly provides simple sugars for the yeasts.

The diastatic power, the Pollak units

To understand the real difference between one malt and another we refer to the enzymatic capacity or diastatic power.

The diastatic power of malt is measured in Pollak units

The Pollak unit is the amount of maltose that is produced from 1000 grams of malted flour in 30 minutes. **The term diastatic therefore indicates the amount of alpha and beta-amylase enzymes present.**

Focaccia with rosemary and coarse salt
When we bake focaccia, we either pierce it with a dough Roller Docker
or we operate a series of pressures with our fingertips on the pizza disc, in or-
der to prevent it from swelling in the oven.

Difference between Malt and Sugar in the dough

As we now know, amylase enzymes are important because they break down complex sugars and create nourishment for yeasts. It is true that many add sugar to the dough, but adding sugar or malt are very different things. Sugar (sucrose) provides nourishment for the yeast in an instant and massive dose, with the addition of malt, instead, the contribution of simple sugars and nutrients for yeasts is more constant and gradual over time, just because in addition to maltose there are enzymes that contribute to the splitting of the starch in the dough, so we feed the yeast gradually during fermentation.

Malt is certainly very important in long leavened doughs, in indirect doughs and cases of flours with low amylase activity (high falling number).
Using malt, a natural additive derived from cereal is added, which gives the product a typical taste and a particular color during cooking.

The doses of malt to be used in the dough

We have certainly understood that the amylase activity of flour is fundamental because it is the process that allows bringing nourishment to the yeasts, but this process of transformation of starch into sugars must last for the whole period of fermentation. Now you understand why I say that adding sugar is not the same thing, sucrose provides immediate "food" but not an enzymatic activity, so it may be fine if you want a short and fast leavening, but in what amount the sucrose should be added? No, I opt for diastatic malt, which has characteristics close to my modus operandi, since I prefer long maturations and I work very often with indirect dough method.
As for the doses to be used here, a new page opens, first of all, it is decided what type of product you want to obtain and then the process that will be applied: direct dough for long leavening, indirect dough and, in this case, with what doses of Biga or Poolish. Having established this, we proceed to consider what type of malt should be used, in fact a malted flour can have 13000 Pollak units, a malt extract in syrup 16000, a concentrated malt extract in syrup 24000 while a powder malt extract obtained from malt extract in syrup has a diastatic capacity of about 8000, therefore very low. It is then added sugar concentrations that are different from malt to malt. In short, how is a dose per product given?

The percentage of malt depends on how the dough is prepared. In long fermentation and indirect methods, the yeast consumes a lot of sugars from the flour. The same happens for leavened products like Panettone and Colomba. In these cases, malt is important to provide extra sugars and enzymes.

On the following table, I am going to indicate the values of malt to be inserted in the dough. Personally, I use malt flour with values of Pollak unit around 18000 and the doses that we find below are for a malted flour of this type.

Dough processing method	Recommended malt percentages referring to the weight of flour
Direct dough method 18/20 hours of leavening	0,2/0,3%
Indirect dough method using a Biga dose of 20%	0,3/0,4% added in the refreshment
Indirect dough method using a Biga dose of 30/40%	0,4/0,5% added in the refreshment
Indirect dough method using a Biga dose of 50/60%	0,5/0,6% added in the refreshment
Indirect dough method using a Biga dose of 60/100%	0,8/% added in the refreshment
Indirect dough method using Poolish	0,3/0,5% added in the refreshment

With these numbers, we have a starting point that, as far as I'm concerned, is already a good thing, but my advice is to experiment to get to the desired result.

Excessive use of diastatic malt can lead to high amylase activity, which can result in water accumulation in pizza dough boxes and sticky dough

FLOURS AND THEIR FUNDAMENTAL CHARACTERISTICS

Flour is the product obtained from the milling and refining of cereals and not cereals, legumes, starch, nuts, and other products, where milling means a process of controlled reduction.

The flour used in bread making is mainly obtained from soft wheat (Triticum Aestivum or Triticum Vulgare), whilst durum wheat (Triticum durum) is used to obtain semolina, whole wheat semolina, and re-milled semolina. Compared to white flour, semolina is granular and has an intense yellow-amber color because it contains carotenoids. It is harder to work with and less extendible than white flour and this is why it is suitable for the production of bread and pasta.

Soft wheat and durum wheat belong to two separate species that form part of the Gramineae family.
Although the two plants are very similar at a structural level, they are not simply two different varieties, but two different species (durum wheat has 28 chromosomes, while soft wheat has 42) and even the proteins present in them are generally different.

Soft wheat flour (soft because the grain breaks easily) has a powdery, indefinite quality to it, with small granules with rounded edges. Durum wheat or durum semolina is made by milling durum, a grain that is difficult to break apart. This grain has sharp edges and the color, which varies depending on the grain used, is transmitted to the finished products.

This is buckwheat, belongs to the family of Polygonaceae. It does not develop gluten as it does not contain Gliadin. Rich in proteins, even comparable to proteins of animal origin.

If used in the dough it is best to combine with strong flours to make up for the lack of gluten.

Flours in the world are divided by their ash content and by their sifting level, which has been carried out after the grinding process.

It is clear that some countries do classify flours by numbers and by matching their ash content, their extraction or sifting degree, whereas in other places or more, like, United States, United Kingdom, flours are described by phrases, or names, which identify their purpose in bread-making.

Knowing the correspondence between the various flours, it is certainly helpful for the preparation of the dough, but we must not forget that to believe that all the flours indicated with the same number or type are equal is an error. The type or the number indicates the milling yield the ash content and how much the flour is sifted, but not the rheological characteristics and the quality of the very same, as this applies for US and UK flours and in those Countries where similar classification methods are adopted; it would be unthinkable to catalog all flours variety with the same name, like for example an all-purpose flour, with an equal values content.

The choice of the type of flour for a dough goes well beyond the milling yield and the ash content.

Italian Flours classification

soft wheat	maximum humidity	Ashes minimum content	Ashes maximum content	Proteins minimum content
Flour type 00	14,50 %	-	0,55 %	9,00 %
Flour type 0	14,50 %	-	0,65 %	11,00 %
Flour type 1	14,50 %	-	0,80 %	12,00 %
Flour type 2	14,50 %	-	0,95 %	12,00 %
whole wheat flour	14,50 %	1,30 %	1,70 %	12,00 %

As we can see the flours in Italy are divided into 00, 0, 1, 2, "*integrale*" (whole wheat flour). These numbers only indicate the grain and its size and are not to be confused with quality, with the ability to absorb water and sustain a long leavening.

German flours classification

Soft wheat	Ashes in milligrams per 100 grams of flour
Flour type 405	<500
Flour type 550	510-630
Flour type 812	640-900
Flour type 1050	910-1200
Flour type 1600	1210-1800
Flour type 1700	<2100

French flours classification

Soft wheat	Ashes in milligrams per 100 grams of flour
Flour type 45	<500
Flour type 55	500-600
Flour type 65	620-750
Flour type 80	750-900
Flour type 110	1000-1200
Flour type 150	>1400

US flour classification

Ashes percentage	US soft wheat flours are called	Protein
~ 0,45 %	Pastry flour	~ 9%
~ 0,55 %	All-purpose flour	~ 11%
~ 0,80 %	High gluten flour	~ 14%
~ 1,10 %	First clear flour	~ 15%
> 1,50 %	White whole wheat	~ 13%

Flours in the world

	Very refined flour					Wholemeal flour
ITALY	00	0		Tipo 1	Tipo 2	integrale
USA	Pastry flour	All-purpose flour		High gluten flour	First clear flour	White whole wheat
UK	Patent flour	Plain flour		Strong bread flour	Brown flour	Wholemeal flour
GERMANY	405	550		812	1050	Vollkorn 1600
FRANCE	45	55	65	80	110	Farine intègral 150
PORTUGAL & SPAIN	45	55	70	80	110	Harina integrale 150
POLAND	Tortowa	Luksusowa		Chlebowa	Sitkowa	Razowa
HOLLAND	Zeeuwse bloem	Patentbloem		Tarwebloem	Gebuilde bloem	Volkorenmeel
CZECH REPUBLIC & SLOVAKIA	Hladká mouka výběrová 00	Hladká mouka		Polohrubá mouka	Hrubá mouka	Celozrnná mouka
ARGENTINA	0000	000		00	0	½
INDIA		Maida/Safed			Atta	Chakki Atta
CHINA		中筋麵粉				小麦面粉

The proteins of the grain of wheat or caryopsis and their importance

Albumins *represent about 9% of the total protein content, soluble in water and saline solutions, found in the outer part of the caryopsis and in the embryo.*
Globulins *represent about 5-7% of the total protein content, located almost exclusively in the germ, they are soluble in saline solutions.*

These proteins are complete in essential amino acids. Unfortunately, being localized in the germ and the pericarp, they are removed during the sifting (milling process). I remind you that wheat germs are rich in lipids and are subject to rancidity, with consequences on the flour and therefore it separates to lengthen the shelf-life of the flours.

Then we have **Gliadins** and **Glutenins** that abound in the endosperm.
However, these proteins, which are present in a large percentage, are qualitatively scarce as they are rich in cysteine, proline, and glycine, but poor in lysine and methionine, which represent the limiting amino acids of cereals.

Glutenins (about 40% of the total) insoluble in water, soluble in acid and base solutions).

Gliadins (about 44% of total proteins) insoluble in water, soluble in alcohol).

The proteins insoluble in water; ***Gliadins and Glutenins,*** *defined as a reserve, are* ***fundamental*** *because they confer bread-making attitude given that they are responsible for gluten formation.* ***Without gluten, it would not be possible to process the pizza dough.***

Indirect dough method with Biga and flour mixed with cereals.

GLUTEN

Mixing water and flour starts the colloidal processes for the union of Gliadin and Glutenin, which give a high degree of stickiness.

Gliadin + Glutenin + water + imparted energy = GLUTIN

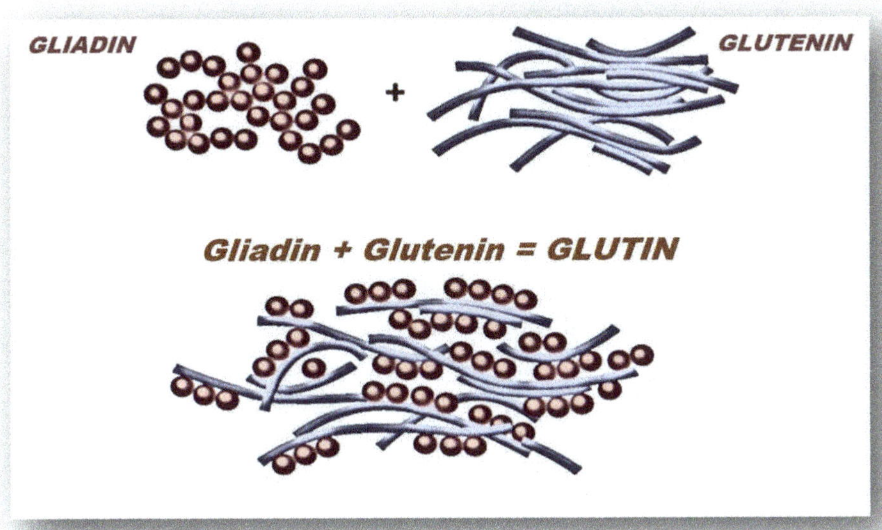

Gliadins

Affects the viscosity of the dough.

The Gliadins in contact with water form a sticky mass and are responsible for the extensibility and viscosity of gluten.

Glutenins

Are responsible for the tenacity and elasticity of the dough.

These two proteins, when added water to the flour and knead, combine with inter-molecular bonds to form gluten.

Gluten is fundamental for the creation of pizza dough

We always hear about gluten and we have just learned that this viscoelastic mesh is the result of a mechanical action that combines two particular proteins with water, where the mechanical action is understood as manual processing or kneading.
Here we understand the importance of insoluble proteins, **Gliadin** and **Glutenin**, in flour. With the presence of the same low, the glutinic mesh is weak, therefore it will produce a dough not suitable for high hydration, or long leavening.

Flours are not all the same, and their protein content has a decisive influence on our doughs. Let's start by saying that, we would have to consider this fact, the leavening hours , do influence what we want, as well as the type of product we are going to achieve; this applies whether we work with non-professional flours, (for example from supermarkets), or whether we rely on professional products specially designed for making pizza.

Also, the percentage of the same proteins present, influences the gluten mesh, in fact, there is strong gluten if the *glutenin* is in a higher dose than the *gliadin*. This data, however, interests us relatively, given that generally the percentage of every single protein on the label is not reported, but the percentage of the sum of all those present.

Gluten and W

Now even in the supermarket, there are bags of flour with the initials W followed by a number, this W is basically used on the technical data sheets of professional flours and indicates the strength of the flour. A high value of W denotes a greater quantity of gluten, this means that the flour will absorb a lot of water, that the dough will be resistant and tenacious and that it will rise slowly because of the meshes of the grid that make up the gluten which will be thick and resistant. On the contrary, a low W is synonymous with flours that may be less hydrated and that will withstand fewer hours of leavening at room temperature R.T.

A very tenacious glutinic mesh does not allow the dough to swell easily and strong pressures are created inside, while an extensible glutinic mesh will easily expand even at low-pressure values.

W 120	Poor and not usable in bread-making flours, suitable for biscuit production
W 120-150	Weak flour not suitable for baking (biscuits, waffles, cakes, béchamel, also used to thicken)
W 160-200	Mediocre strength flour suitable for bread-making with direct dough method (biscuits, sweets, bread, biscuits)
W 210-260	Medium-high strength flours, suitable for direct bread-making (French bread, sandwiches, pizza with short leavening, sheet pan pizza pan, all of which absorb more or less 53-57%)
W 270-340	Medium-high strength flours suitable for direct and indirect doughs method (classic bread, croissant, pizza, babà, long-leavened pastry, absorb 55 to 80% water)
W 350 and above	Force flours suitable for doughs that require long leavening, suitable pizza peel roman style, Biga, Poolish, flour with W 400 can also absorb 100% of water

But how much can a flour rise based on its W value?

To find out, let's see the following page

Relationship between W (force) and leavening hours

(indicative data using hydration, yeast doses, and ideal temperatures. For more precise values always refer to the datasheet of the producer)

Flour strength (W)	Possible leavening hours at R.T.
W >380	15/20 hours
W >320	11/14 hours
W >280	8/10 hours
W >220	2/6 hours
W >180	1/ 2 hours

The strength of the flour is certainly the parameter most taken into account by the Pizzaioli and I would also say the simplest since based on this value you can decide hydration and fermentation times.

Spelt is a herbaceous plant of the family Gramineae of which there are three different species: Triticum monococcum commonly called "einkorn", Triticum dicoccum called commonly "spelled", Triticum spelta commonly called "spelled great."
Spelt has had a remarkable success thanks to the fact that it grows well in poor soils and it is very resistant to cold. Spelt is different from wheat because it remains shrouded in husk after threshing.
Spelt is one of the oldest species of wheat, dating back to the Neolithic era. It contains Gliadin, so it develops gluten. It contains a fair amount of protein and gives a very special taste to the dough.

From the table on the previous page, it is clear that each flour must be used according to the established hours of rising. For example, if we want an espresso product and we decide to prepare a pizza in 4 or 6 hours, without maturation, we must necessarily use a weak flour with a W around 220 (short processes without maturation are always indigestible in my opinion).

Let's try now to figure out how we can regulate ourselves if we don't have the W-value available.

The W is a value that is obtained by an instrumental test is tied to the proteins of the flour, but it is not really correct to say that many proteins correspond to a high W since the strength also depends on the type of the same present. But let's not be afraid, in an approximate way, **the proteins indicated on the label on a _very refined flour_ generally reflect those suitable for bread-making**, this is because the essential proteins are largely removed in the phase of sifting.
Let's say that if on the flour label we read that the total proteins are 14% then we are dealing with definitely strong flour, if we read that the total proteins are 10%, we are faced with a weak flour. *As an indication, each percentage point corresponds to a variation of W equal to 50.*
You may have noticed that I wrote: "the proteins indicated on the label on a _very refined flour_ generally reflect those suitable for bread-making". I did it with good reason since the less refined flours generally have a higher protein content than the most sifted flours and the reason is that most of the essential proteins, those called albumins and globulins are found in the bran parts and the germ, so the less flour is refined the more they will be present, only that this type of protein is not influential in the formation of the gluten mesh and therefore has little influence on strength. **In conclusion, the proteins found in the most refined flours are only those suitable for the formation of the glutinic mesh.**

Wholemeal flour generally has more protein than refined flour, on the other hand, it also contains proteins present in the external teguments and in the germ, but making a 100% wholemeal dough is virtually impossible for the purposes of pizza shaping.

The following table shows the approximate correspondence between proteins and W

Flour strength	Proteins
W 90-130	9-10 %
W 130-180	10-11 %
W 180-230	11-12 %
W 230-280	12-13 %
W 280-340	13-14 %
W 340-400	14-15 %

The strength of the flour, its water absorption, the hydration of the dough

The strength of the flour, therefore, the W, helps us to understand how much we can hydrate a dough. How many times do you get a soft and a hard dough using the same doses of water and flour? This depends precisely on the glutinic mesh that flours can develop. A high W gives rise to strong gluten who can absorb a lot of water, which is why to make pizza with high hydration, it is essential to use strong flours. The pizza peel roman style, which requires 80% hydration, must be prepared with flours rich in Manitoba where the W varies from 350 to 400.

Flour with cereal mix. When we knead with this type of flour, it becomes important to perform the stop & go technique. Let the flour soak in the water for 20 or 30 minutes in order to give it the opportunity to hydrate properly before proceeding to the actual dough.
This technique is also used with wholemeal or semolina flours.

Gluten-free flours

| Rice flour |
| Sorghum flour |
| Amaranth flour |
| Corn flour |
| Millet flour |
| Buckwheat flour |
| Chickpea flour |
| Chestnut flour (suitable for desserts) |
| Soya flour |
| Tapioca flour |
| Quinoa flour |
| Teff flour (white and red) |
| Lupin flour |
| Hemp flour |
| Coconut flour (suitable for cakes) |
| Chia flour |
| Beans flour |
| Broad bean flour |
| Lentil Flour |
| Chickpea flour |
| Grape seed flour |
| Peanut flour |
| Walnut flour |
| Hazelnut flour |
| Almond flour (suitable for cakes) |
| Peas flour |
| Coffee flour |
| Potato Flour |
| Carob flour (suitable for cakes) |
| Banana flour (suitable for cakes) |
| Pumpkin flour |

There is another value to take into consideration when kneading, it is **the P/L**

The P/L is a relationship between tenacity and extensibility of flour, this data is obtained instrumentally, is reported together with the W in the datasheet of a professional flour. Without going into detail, I bring the optimal values to the table.

Optimum P/L ratios

The P/L ratio	
Tenacious flours for baking	P/L > 0,7
Very extensible flours	P/L < 0,4
Balanced flours	P/L 0,5-0,6

For example, a dough with flour that has a ratio P/L > 0.7 indicates a very tenacious product and difficult to knead, provides a little developed bread with heavy and compact crumb, if instead, we use a flour with a ratio P/L<03, for example, we are using a flour that will be spring, extensible, sticky during processing, which gives rise to bread with little volume and flattened the glutinic mesh breaks and cannot retain the carbon dioxide.

When choosing a flour, it is essential to consider W and P/L. In the case of non-professional flours, P/L is not shown on the label, so we just have to ask the manufacturer and if we are unable to find this information, the only solution is to run some tests.

YEAST DOSES TO BE ADDED TO THE DOUGHS

Let's get into a very much debated topic: the doses of yeast to use.

The strength of the flour, the rising hours and temperature, the dough hydration and the desired product are the factors to consider when deciding the amount of yeast for a dough.

Very simply, however, if we adopt the concept of maturation as I have expressed it in this book, everything becomes very simple, in fact, we will use for a traditional pizza 1 or 1.5 grams of yeast per kg of flour in summer and 2 or 2.5 grams per kg of flour in winter. This is if the maturation starts from 18 to 24 hours.

For those who want to use different working times, there are a couple of formulas that allow you to calculate the approximate amount of yeast needed for each type of dough, deciding the hours of rising, the rising temperature and hydration.

The following table indicates the flour to be used according to the leavening hours we choose.

Flour strength (W)	Possible leavening hours at R.T.
W >380	15/20 hours
W >320	11/14 hours
W >280	8/10 hours
W >220	2/6 hours
W >180	1/ 2 hours

The doses we get from the formulas are related to direct doughs of traditional round pizza, are not suitable for the calculation of the yeast for pizza pan or Naples style pizza (Neapolitan pizza), **all doses are related to fresh yeast**.

The leavening is influenced by many factors, just think that the pH alone makes it vary, if for example, you have ever kneaded with milk (some types of sheet pan pizza or bread) you will have noticed that the leavening slows down and this it is due precisely to the more basic pH that derives from it, moreover the temperature has an exponential effect within a certain range and an almost linear effect in another until a certain point where there is a drop in the leavening until inhibition. Fermentation is also influenced by the presence of sugars (glycolysis), salt and hydration. To use formulas, you must reduce many variables and remain in the working range. It is, in fact, useless to enter values such as 40 hours of leavening if a flour supports at most 20, how absurd it is to decide a fermentation at 3 °C.

First formula (related to fresh yeast)

In this formula I took into consideration an exponential trend of leavening from 5°C, I obtained a constant K from the logarithm and considering that if the temperature, hydration and leavening time increase the doses of yeast must decrease, I proceeded with a division.

We assume the coefficients to be included in the calculation, which is **K=100.000**

K = 100.000 (coefficients)

- i = % hydration (percentage hydration)

- T^2 = (square leavening temperature)

- t = leavening time expressed in hours

(K) divided by (i), quotient divided by ($T^{2)}$, new quotient divided by (t)

$$\frac{\dfrac{\frac{k}{i}}{T^2}}{t} = \text{\% of fresh yeast per kg of flour}$$

example let's assume hydration of 56% at a temperature of 24 °C and 16 hours of leavening

100.000: 56: 576: 16 = 0.19% of yeast per kg or about 2 grams per kg of flour. If you opt for 4 hours of leavening, you have to consider that you need a less strong flour that will be hydrated for example to 54%, we will get a result of about 8 grams of fresh yeast per kg of flour.

Second formula (related to fresh yeast)

The first consideration of the following formula is that it derives its quantity of yeast related to a liter of water, therefore the value obtained must be multiplied by the quantity of water to be used in the mixture. In this formulation we assume the coefficients to be included in the calculation, which is **8; 4; 20;**

$$\frac{8}{leavening\ hours} \times (4) \times \frac{20}{leavening\ temperature} = grams\ of\ yeast\ per\ litre$$

As mentioned, we get the amount of yeast to be added to a liter of water. If for example the hydration will be 55% and we refer to 10 kg of flour, the result will be multiplied by 5.5, which will be the liters used in the dough. If water values lower than one liter is used instead, for example, 700 gr., Remember to multiply by 0.7.

More general yeast doses (related to fresh Yeast)

The doses of yeast vary from about 0.1% to 3% depending on the type of product, the hours of leavening and the temperature, all, as always, related to the strength of the flour.
Doses of yeast such as 2.5 or 3% are often used for sheet pan pizza or such products.

Yeast and the differences between the types on the market

Saccharomyces cerevisiae is the strain that has been chosen for commercial yeast because it has characteristics that favor rapid gas production.
Cake Yeast, also known as **wet**, **fresh**, or **compressed yeast**, is widely used in Italy, the advantage in the processing is linked to the fact that it is practically alive and does not need to reawaken so it immediately enters into synergy with the dough.
Cake Yeast can be **added directly** to dry ingredients, can be **dissolved in liquids** before using, is very versatile and performs well in all your recipes.
But Cake yeast is currently sold in limited areas, it also needs to be stored in the refrigerator and has a limited shelf life.

There are two alternative solutions: the **Active Dry Yeast** and e the **Instant Yeast**

Active Dry Yeast has a larger granule and needs to be dissolved in water before using it.
It's a living organism that is dormant until it is dissolved in a small amount of lukewarm water (about 35/40 °C, and often you need to add sugar). It is then added to the rest of the ingredients. Active dry yeast is typically sold in individual packets or small jars.

Instant Yeast has a finer texture and can be mixed right into the dry ingredients. The only precaution is that it should not come in direct contact with cold temperatures, so if you use cold water you must add the instant yeast after water and flour have started to be mixed.

Doses conversions method.

Although it is best to follow the conversion ratio provided by the manufacturer, you can refer to the following values:

To convert *from fresh yeast to active dry yeast,* multiply the fresh quantity by 0.4.

To convert *from fresh yeast to instant dry yeast,* multiply the fresh quantity by 0.33.

In other word, Active dry yeast can be used at 40% of the weight of fresh yeast and instant dry yeast can be used at 33% of the weight of fresh yeast. Cake yeast (fresh yeast) has been used in all the recipes provided by me in this book, you can refer to these values for conversion.

The percentages of Biga and Poolish to be used in the doughs

Since I said to treat Biga and Poolish as if they were yeast, I can indicate the doses I used for this preferment according to the desired product.

Pizza type	Biga and Poolish percentage
Round traditional Pizza	Biga from 15 to 30%, Poolish from 20 to 25%
Pizza Neapolitan style	Biga from 35 to 50%, Poolish 30% (Yung, max. 6 ore)
Pizza peel roman style	Biga from 65 to 80%
Sheet pan Pizza	Biga from 40 to 50%, Poolish 25% (Yung max. 6 ore
Pizza Gourmet	Biga from 60 %

We have not to forget that:

$$Total\ dough = Biga + Refreshment$$

The greater the amount of preferment, the sooner the final dough is put in the fridge.

Sodium chloride (NaCl), commonly known as SALT

Its addition to the dough has multiple functions: it improves the organoleptic characteristics, whitens the crumb, performs a slight antiseptic action reducing secondary fermentation, gives a more pronounced color to the edge, increases the crunchiness and also determines an increase in the quality of gluten improving the rheological characteristics.

Salt effects on gluten

Since gliadin is less soluble in salted water, the addition of salt gives rise to more short-fiber gluten, which makes the dough more compact, the salt then reinforces the gluten, in fact with the addition of NaCl, there's an increase in the alveograph parameters W as well as a decrease in water absorption due to the dehydration of gluten, an increase in development time and an increase in the stability of the dough.

In reality, the effects of adding salt to a dough, as far as rheological characteristics are concerned, also depending on the protein content of the flour.

Thanks to Chopin's alveograph, you can see the instrumental test of dough with two different doses of added salt. If I reported the instrumental proof on a chart, I would get a situation like the one illustrated below. It can clearly be seen that an excessive dose of salt would make the dough too rigid, while we have an excellent between 2.5% and 5%. However, we will shortly see that salt has not the only effect on proteins, but also on yeast, so we will evaluate and see later on the dose to be used precisely according to the effect on the yeast.

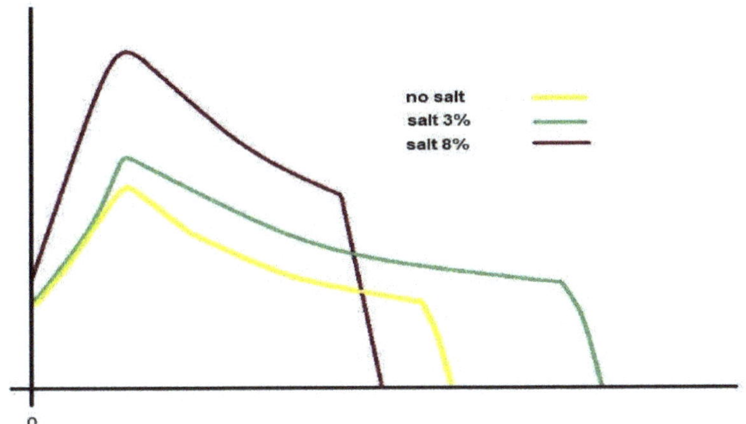

Salt effects on yeast

The osmotic pressure of cells immersed in a hypertonic solution is indicated as cellular plasmolysis.

"What big words!" You'll say, don't be afraid, it's not that complicated.

Osmosis is a phenomenon in which water moves from a less concentrated solution to a more concentrated solution through a semi-permeable membrane and the Saccharomyces Cerevisiae, commonly known as baker's yeast, is a single-celled eukaryote that has this type of membrane. If a cell is placed in a saline solution (a molecule that cannot pass through the cell) the cell will lose water, in which case it is said that the cell is immersed in a hypertonic solution.

In short, there is cellular dehydration.

The process can also be described as **plasmolysis** and it is the process caused by osmosis in which the cells in hypertonic solution undergo a reduction in volume (dehydration), with a consequent detachment of the plasma membrane of the cell wall, bringing the cell even to death.

Finally, we have the answer to the much-quoted phrase "salt kills the yeast", and this is why yeast and salt must not come into direct contact.

Let us remember that even sugar changes the osmotic pressure, only that it does so in a lesser way and at higher percentages of concentration, but also sugar can kill the cell: too much sugar slows the leavening.

We can say that salt has a modulating function in fermentation. This is also the reason why in summer it is used in larger doses.

If dissolved in water, the salt comes into contact with the yeast and should, therefore, be added after a few minutes of mixing.

Fine salt is used in the dough.

In summer, if the temperatures are too high, it is advisable to increase the doses of salt to slow down the fermentation.

Salt effects on yeast CO2 production

Several experiments have been carried out on this subject and it has been demonstrated that by increasing the concentration of sodium chloride (NaCl) in the dough, the yeast decreases the respiratory activity, thus decreasing the production of carbon dioxide responsible for the swelling. The graph shows the results of an experiment carried out with two respective additions of NaCl. The lower CO_2 production at each step is noted, respectively from 0.048 ml CO_2/min to 0.028 ml CO_2/min and finally to 0.023 ml CO_2/min in the third case.

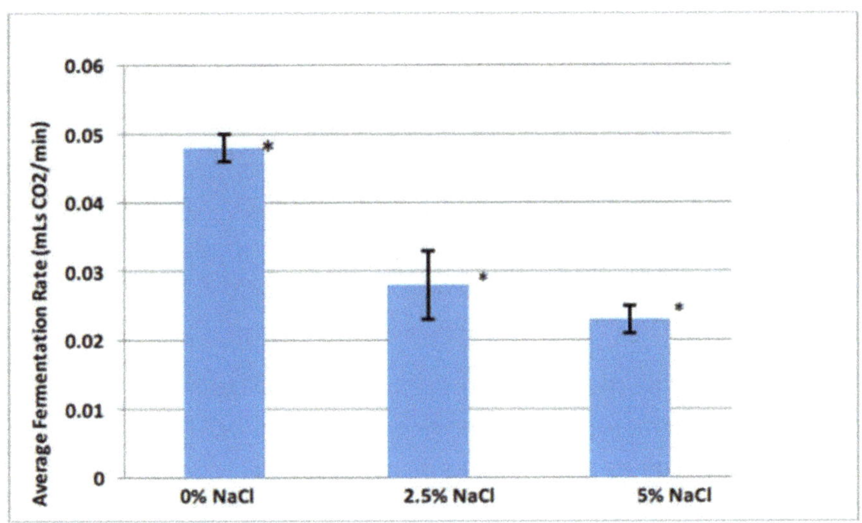

(Shavitz, 2015)

It seems that very low doses of NaCl are however favorable to the activity of the yeast, we are talking about doses around 0.5%, while excessive quantities, such as 5%, are however to be avoided.

Salt effects on amylase. activity

The amylase activity is influenced by the presence of the salt, on the other hand, if the salt influences the proteins, it can be considered that it also affects the enzymatic activities.
It has experimented that up to concentrations of 1% sodium chloride the amylase activity reaches its optimum, beyond this threshold it begins to decrease.
It is also true that high concentrations of salt decrease the activity of water, resulting in a decrease in enzymatic activity.

Salt doses in the pizza dough

The salt amounts to use must take into account the effects they have on the dough, the yeast and the amylase activity.

Salt should be added at the rate of 2% or 2.5%, but in summer you can get to 2.8% even 3% (limit case).

How to add salt to the dough

If you try to sprinkle salt over the crumbled yeast you can witness its water loss, that is its dehydration, this as a proof of what previously said, ***therefore the addition of salt is generally carried out after flour, yeast, and water have started to amalgamate:***
Personally, I insert it after 6 to 8 minutes at speed one of the mixer. The working methods can still be customized while respecting the basic guidelines: the yeast does not come into direct contact with the salt.

Salt and preferment

Salt, as we have seen, has the ability to inactivate microorganisms, this is one of the reasons why it is not used in preferment (Biga or Poolish). The preferment must be able to give free rein to the reproduction of yeasts and lactobacilli and their fermentation, on the other hand, there is already a lot of competition from the nutritional point of view between yeasts and LAB.

EXTRA-VIRGIN OLIVE OIL (EVO)

The extra virgin olive oil is undoubtedly the best fat to use on our pizzas, both raw at the end of cooking and in the dough.

The extra virgin olive oil not only has a characteristic taste, which varies from the area of origin of the olive and the harvest season but also has different nutritional qualities.

It counteracts the accumulation of LDL cholesterol, harmful to the body, but it does not affect the HDL cholesterol, the good one, is, therefore, able to purify the blood from the waste of fat and contributes to the prevention of cardiovascular risk.

It has a balanced composition because it contains the ideal ratio between unsaturated and polyunsaturated fats, in particular between two slightly special fatty acids, linoleic acid, and alpha-linolenic acid, called "essential" because the body is not able to produce them on its own.

It fights free radicals thanks to the strong antioxidant power of vitamin E (tocopherol) and various phenolic compounds, all molecules capable of protecting our body from premature aging by combating free radicals.

It is a natural protector of the liver. Thanks to its strong antioxidant properties, it slows down the action of toxins derived from exposure to pollution and chemical substances present in the environment.

Olive oil relieves inflammation and helps protect liver cells, it is also considered the most digestible one thanks to the marked choleretic function or excitation of the biliary function. The function of bile is to emulsify fats thus allowing the attack of pancreatic lipase on triglycerides (with the formation of free fatty acids, mono, and glycerides) and therefore their absorption in the form of micelles.

In not so recent experiments, about fifty years ago, it had demonstrated how olive oil has a marked choleretic and cholagogue activity (the terms cholagogues and choleretic refer, respectively, to the ability to stimulate the bile flow towards the intestine and the secretion of bile from liver cells); there are also some spices that have both properties, such as turmeric and some vegetables, such as Chelidonium, artichoke, taraxacum (dandelion), absinthe (which is a distillate) and others.

In conclusion, olive oil, due to its effectiveness on the activity of the gallbladder, promotes the digestive phase of lipids due to their emulsifying action by bile.

The characteristics of the olive oil studied were also found in other oils but with minor effects, in order, there were peanut oil, sesame oil, corn oil.

OIL in the dough

The fats are not essential for making the dough, unlike water, yeast, salt, and flour. As we have seen, oil is an improvement but not essential, in fact, many pizzerias do not use EVO, especially, is not added to the Neapolitan pizza dough. Its use from an organoleptic point of view removes gumminess to the product. Reading what is said about Neapolitan pizza, it must be soft, elastic and easily foldable into a "booklet".
I personally use olive oil also in the Neapolitan dough. The reason is simple: in addition to the improved characteristics of the fats, the oil has great importance from an organoleptic point of view.

Crunchy or fragrant

Extra virgin olive oil, due to its shortening effect, that is the loss of the extensibility of the mass due to its particular composition of unsaturated fatty acids, does not give crunchiness but fragrance, while the seed oils give crunchiness. However, small doses of seed oil are not able to give acceptable results, it is not by chance that they are used in greater quantities than the extra virgin olive oil. For example, products such as breadsticks can contain up to 15% of seed oil.

Oil Smoke Point

The smoke point is meant as the temperature at which a heated food fat begins to release volatile substances that can be harmful or even carcinogenic to humans.
If by heating oil, it reaches a certain temperature, it will begin to produce smoke in a continuous way well before it begins to boil, at this temperature, there is the point of smoke. In practice, triglycerides are separated into fatty acids and glycerol, the latter then turns into acrolein, an irritant substance that is toxic to the liver and probably carcinogenic to humans.

Various seed oils have different smoke points and should not be used, especially if poured on the pizza before it is baked.

Below is an indicative table on the smoke points of the main oils used:

Extra virgin olive oil	smoke point 210 °C
Peanut oil	smoke point 180 °C
Corn oil	smoke point 160 °C
Sunflower oil	smoke point 130 °C

It is important to choose the right fats during cooking, for example, in the pizza marinara, or at least the only tomato pizzas without mozzarella, they include a drizzle of oil before baking, in order to prevent the tomato water from evaporating and leaving a dry pizza for the dehydration of the tomato itself. In these cases, the extra virgin olive oil is essential, as it has the highest smoke point, moreover it has a more marked taste.

Oils with a different chemical composition oxidize differently. Those rich in polyunsaturated fats, such as corn oil or soybean oil, degrade more rapidly than those rich in monounsaturated fats, such as olive oil or peanut oil, which are mainly composed of oleic acid, also extra virgin olive oil, not having been purified, contains molecules that act as antioxidants delaying degradation.

When to pour oil into the dough.

The lipids interact with starch and gluten, for this to happen it is right to claim that their use should be placed at the beginning of processing, but not in close contact with the yeasts. If the oil is added to the kneading machine when the dough is almost ready, as often, this is the case, there is a risk of lengthening the preparation time, given that lipids tend to create separations that, even if later recomposed, definitely lengthen the times. Beyond the scientific explanations, if the gluten mesh is well-formed and we add all the oil we notice an immediate disintegration and separation into pieces of the same dough, which will present difficulties in recomposing itself, due to the emulsifying effect generated by the oil.

The doses of extra virgin olive oil to be used in the dough

Indicatively I report the most commonly used values of extra virgin olive oil in a dough:

Classical round Pizza	2-3%
Sheet Pan Pizza	5%
Focaccia Genovese	7-10%

For seed oil, the doses are generally higher than the extra virgin olive oil, but there is no real percentage, it is a question of understanding the product you want to make. Often I happened to find pizza makers who do not use olive oil because of its cost, especially in the Caribbean it is not used for this reason, but the replacement with seed oils does do not bring the same characteristics.

PIZZA BAKING

Baking in the pizzeria sector is an extremely important factor and not often considered, as is the **oven,** which for a pizzeria is the life of the same restaurant.
An oven that cools quickly due to repeated full baking, that is if the pizzas cover all the free points on the oven floor, creates a number of drawbacks:

- pizzas undercooked on the base (not optimal product)
- waiting times getting longer for customers
- the consequent reduction of the seats (the customers at the tables do not replace each other)

The oven is the real engine of the Pizzeria, an undersized oven does not allow you to satisfy customers, an oven that cools down because it is of poor quality does not let you work in the right way, an undersized oven has a low output of pizzas/hour and does not allow you to improve the Pizzeria if clients increase in number.

Thanks to the oven take place the cooking

Cooking gives life to a series of chemical-physical processes that are extremely important and involve not only the organoleptic qualities of the finished product but also those inherent in the digestibility of the product itself.

What happens when baking pizza

We must consider that temperature is fundamental for:
- *yeasts and microorganisms*
- *enzymes*
- *starch gelatinization*
- *denaturation of proteins*
- *Maillard reaction*

Chemical-physical transformations during the baking phase

As soon as we bake there is a rapid increase in activity by the yeasts until their total inactivation, there is an increase in enzyme activity, the gelatinization of starch, the evaporation of volatile substances, the denaturation of proteins, the reaction of Maillard.

In the initial phase, there is a drastic increase in fermentation, with the production of CO_2, ethyl alcohol, lactic acid, acetic acid, and other organic acids.
The fast production of carbon dioxide causes an immediate expansion, which in the pizza mainly concerns the edge or crust.
This happens in the passage of temperature that goes between 28 and 40 °C, then there is a decrease in activity by the yeasts that are definitively inhibited between 50 and 60 °C.
At the latter temperature starch gelatinization also begins, with a consequent increase in enzymatic activity which finding a compromised starch has fertile soil resulting in a large production of simpler sugars, dextrins, maltose, glucose.
Beta-amylase catalyzes up to about 85°C, alpha-amylase, being more resistant, it continues its process up to just under 100°C.

Between 60°C and 70°C also begins the denaturation of proteins, through this process the proteins lose their original biological function and tend to coagulate, cooking involves the loss of water and the stiffening of the glutinic mesh.

Denaturation also causes an increase in proteolysis, since protease resists like beta-amylase up to 80/85 °C.

As the temperature rises from 90°C to 100°C all the water released begins to evaporate, the edge dries and begins the concomitant cessation of gelatinization of starch.

At these temperatures, all substances with an evaporation point of less than 100°C, such as ethyl alcohol and the aromatic substances formed during fermentation, also begin to evaporate.

Above 100/110°C, the caramelization of the residual sugars present in the dough begins and *Maillard's reaction* takes place around 140°C.

The Maillard reaction is a complex series of phenomena that occurs following the interaction between sugars and proteins, this rather complex and heterogeneous reaction leads to the formation of different substances such as melanoid, which have a characteristic color.

Since it is a reaction between carbohydrates and proteins, it is clear that it will be optimal if both are present in large quantities. The Maillard reaction that occurs during the cooking of the pizza involves sugars and proteins, which cause the typical coloring of the edge. In addition to coloring, it also gives a characteristic taste to the crust, thanks to the caramelized sugar.

Maillard's reaction in pizza involves the parts that are not covered with topping, generally, only in those areas, there is such a rise in temperature as to make the phenomenon possible.

Soft pizza, very hot oven and fast baking

To obtain a soft pizza, we start with a more hydrated dough that also cooks very quickly because the pizza will be cooked before all the water has evaporated. The oven must be very hot. The Neapolitan pizza is soft because of the high hydration and of the high cooking temperature, followed by a minimum stay in the oven, ranging from 50 to 60 seconds, in which case the oven generally has a deck (floor) temperature of about 400 °C and the dome at about 450 °C.

Crispy pizza, slow baking, less hot oven

To get a crispy pizza, on the contrary, you need a longer cooking time, so a less hot oven to give the possibility to all the liquids to evaporate. For a crunchy pizza, it is good to shape the pizza ball so that they remain very thin, in fact, a very flat pizza is easier to be crunchy, not only, but if it is too thick and has small alveolation becomes hard, almost difficult to cut. It is also possible to change the quality of the product by changing the cooking position, for example by staying away from the flame or in the oven mouth (cooking in the "mouth").

BAKING IS ONE OF THE FUNDAMENTAL STEPS TO OBTAIN A QUALITY PRODUCT.

PIZZA DOUGHS RECIPES

In this chapter, I am going to give some recipes for making both direct and indirect doughs

Before we get into the reading it's important to know:

- with R.T. (room temperature) I refer to a controlled temperature between 19 °C and 21 °C.

- Since all recipes are made with fresh yeast, it is possible to convert the type of yeast used, referring to page 92.

- When it is recommended to put the dough on the workbench to observe a resting period, it should be worked as explained on page 39.

- The malt flour used in the recipes is 18.000 Pollak units.

ingredients:

- Italian Flour type 0 W 280/320
- 56% of water
- 2,5% of salt
- 2,5% of extra virgin olive oil
- 0,15% of fresh yeast

Procedure:

- mix flour and water for 10 minutes, leaving 10% of the total water aside
- give few folds to the "autolysis dough" and place it in a dough container box, cover with a lid or food film and let it rest for 12 hours at 19/20 °C
- put the "autolysis dough" back in the mixer, add the water left aside with the dissolved yeast inside, one minute later the mixer was turned on, pour the oil and after 5 minutes the salt. The dough is kneaded until is smooth and detached from walls of the mixer bowl
- extract the dough and let it rest for around 20 minutes on the workbench covered
- shape the pizza dough balls around 200/210 grams and let's put ten per box
- let it leaven for about 2 hours to R.T.
- then put everything in a fridge at 3 °C for 12 hours minimum
- Remove the dough from the fridge and let it leaven at room temperature for about 4 or 5 hours (time suitable for this flour). When leavening is complete, the dough balls will have to touch each other

If the size of the pizza loaves is 200/210 grams or more, it is better to put 10 dough balls per box like in the picture. When they are leavened, they will touch and it will be easier to remove them without ruining them.

Direct dough method using medium strength flour, and maturation in the refrigerator after the formation of the pizza dough balls

Ingredients:

- Italian Flour type 0 W 240/260
- 55% of water
- 0,3% of malt flour
- 2,5% of salt
- 2,5 of extra virgin olive oil
- 0,15% of fresh yeast

Procedure:

- mix the ingredients, remember to knead until the dough is smooth and detached from walls of the mixer bowl
- extract the dough and let it rest for about 20 minutes on the workbench covered
- shape the pizza dough balls around 200/210 grams
- let it ferment for about 1 or 2 hours at R.T.
- place the pizza dough boxes in the fridge at 3 °C for 24/48 hours (remember to swap the dough box positions after the first few hours)
- Remove the dough from the fridge and let it leaven at room temperature for about 3 or 4 hours (time suitable for this flour). When leavening is complete, the dough balls will have to touch each other

Here we see how the dough must be before being worked.
Note the correct fermentation of the loaves.
This is the result of proper leavening.

Ingredients:

- Italian Flour type 0 W 220
- 54% of water
- 0,3% of malt flour
- 2,8% of salt
- 3% extra virgin olive oil
- 0,15% of fresh yeast

Procedure:

- mix the ingredients, remember to knead until the dough is smooth and detached from walls of the mixer bowl
- remove the dough from the mixer and fold it before placing it in a large dough container twice or triple the dough itself, cover it with a lid or food film and let it rest 10 minutes at R.T.
- place the dough container in a fridge at 3 °C for 24/48 hours
- remove the container and bring the dough to about 18 °C or until you can work it to make the pizza dough balls
- form pizza dough balls around 200/210 grams and leave them to rise for about 3 hours at room temperature before use (time suitable for this flour)
- it is possible to select only the quantity of dough we need, the rest can remain in the refrigerator, not exceeding 48 hours

Pizza Margherita made with direct dough and mass maturation of 36 hours in a cold room at 3 °C, baked in a wood-burning oven at 400°C.

Direct dough method with superior medium strength flour and mass maturation without the use of refrigerator

Ingredients:

- Italian Flour type 0 W 280/320
- 55% of water
- 2,8 % of salt
- 3% of extra virgin olive oil
- 0,15% of fresh yeast

Procedure:

- mix water, flour, and **salt**, leaving about 15% water apart
- give few folds to the "autolysis dough" and place it in a dough container box, cover with a lid or food film and let it rest at a controlled temperature of 19/21 °C for 24 hours
- put everything back in the mixer, add the water left aside with the dissolved yeast inside, one minute later the mixer was turned on, pour the oil. The dough is kneaded until is smooth and detached from walls of the mixer bowl
- extract the dough and let it rest for about 20 minutes on the workbench covered, after which make dough pizza balls around 200/210 grams or desired weight
- let then the dough leaven for about 5/6 hours at R.T. before using it

Note how the dough in the photo is flatter than those made with Biga.

<u>Direct dough method with a mix of different flours.</u> *Using the procedure indicated on page 60 (stop & go)*

Ingredients:

- 70% Italian Flour type 0
- 30% wholemeal flour or semolina or multi cereals flours (30% of these flours are already a very good percentage)
- 2,8% of salt
- 3% extra virgin olive oil
- 0,3% of malt flour
- 0,15% of fresh yeast

Example of dough with 10 kg of flour whose hydration is the sum of the partial hydration given to the individual flours

- 7000 gr. flour 0 W 260 to which we apply a 54% hydro (3780 gr. water)
- 3000 gr. of wholemeal to which we apply a 60% hydro (1800 gr. of water)
- Total flours 10,000 grams total water 5580 grams
- 280 gr. of salt on the total
- 300 gr. extra virgin olive oil
- 30 gr. of malt
- 15 gr. fresh yeast

Procedure:

- insert the wholemeal in the mixer and pour 60% of the total water
- run the mixer at speed 1 for about two minutes, and perform a 30-minute machine stop (stop & go)
- after the stop & go finish the dough by inserting the other ingredients and restarting the mixer
- apply one of the methods of maturation seen so far

Semolina, wholemeal flours, multi cereals flour or otherwise not very refined flours, have a variable absorption that varies from 58% to even 65%. The range I have indicated is quite accurate, I personally evaluate by observing the product. This is where experience comes into play.

Here is a direct dough method with wholemeal flour. The reason I put 8 loaves per box is that these doughs require larger pizza balls in order to be able to shape them easily.
240-grams dough pizza balls in the photo.

On the side a Pizza Margherita made with this wholemeal dough.

Ingredients

- the flour used in the refreshment is: Italian flour type 0 W 300/320
- 56 % of water (based on the total dough)
- 2,5% of salt
- 2,5% of extra virgin olive oil
- 0,5% of malt (added on refreshment)
- 0,05% of fresh yeast (added on refreshment)

Example of dough

- 10.000 gr. of flour
- 5600 gr. of water
- 250 gr. of salt
- 250 gr. of extra virgin olive oil
- 50 gr. of malt flour
- 5 gr. of fresh yeast

Biga

- Italian flour type 0 (all-purpose flour) W 320/350
- 44% of water
- 1% of fresh yeast
- 25% of Biga for this dough will be a Biga of 2500 gr. of flour, with 1100 gr. of water and 25 gr. of yeast

Refreshment

- 7.500 gr. of flour   (10.000 – 2500: (total flour – Biga flour)
- 4500 gr. of water   (5600 – 1100: total water – Biga water)
- 250 gr. of salt
- 250 gr. of extra virgin olive oil
- 50 gr. of malt flour
- 5 gr. of fresh yeast

Procedure:

- prepare the Biga with the indicated doses and let it ferment for 18/20 hours at 18 °C.
- when the Biga is ready, proceed with the refreshment: put the flour, water, yeast, and malt in the mixer, turn it on and about one or two minutes later add the Biga after having divided it into smaller parts, then pour the oil and 5 or 6 minutes later add salt and knead until the dough is smooth and detached from walls of the mixer bowl
- extract the dough and let it rest for about 20 minutes on the workbench covered, after which make dough pizza balls around 200/210 grams or desired weight
- let it leaven for about 1 or 2 hours at R.T.
- place the pizza dough balls in a fridge at 3 °C for 24/48 hours (remember to swap the dough box positions after the first few hours)
- Remove the dough from the fridge and let it leaven at room temperature for about 4 or 5 hours. When leavening is complete, the dough balls will have to touch each other

In the picture, you can see the typical thrust that the Biga generates in leavening
The 200-gram loaves touch each other so we're ready to shape them.
To manage this type of dough you need to give it extra attention.
The use of Biga provides us with a superior product, but let's not forget the maturation.

You can also add spices, such as curry, to the mixture. In the photo, 1% of curry has been added to the previous page's dough.
Underneath the pizza with curry dough topped with mozzarella fior di latte, asparagus, zucchini and grated boiled egg.

Ingredients

- the flour used in the refreshment is: Italian flour type 0 W 280/320
- 63% of water (based on the total dough)
- 3% of salt
- 1,5% of extra virgin olive oil
- 0,5% of malt flour (added in refreshments)
- 0,1% of fresh yeast

Example of dough

- 10.000 gr. of flour
- 6300 gr. of water
- 300 gr. of salt
- 150 gr. of extra virgin olive oil
- 50 gr. of malt flour
- 10 gr. of fresh yeast

Biga

- Italian flour type 0 (all-purpose flour) W 320/350
- 44 % of water
- 1 % of fresh yeast
- 40% of Biga for this dough will be a Biga of 4000 gr. of flour, with 1760 gr. of water and 40 gr. of fresh yeast

Refreshment

- 6000 gr. of flour   (10.000 – 4000: total flour – Biga flour)
- 4540 gr. of water   (6300 – 1760: total water – Biga water)
- 300 gr. of salt
- 150 gr. of extra virgin olive oil
- 50 gr. of malt
- 10 gr. of fresh yeast

This recipe does not follow the AVPN disciplinary of the Neapolitan pizza.

Procedure

- prepare the Biga with the doses indicated and let it ferment 18/20 hours at 18 °C.
- when the Biga is ready you can proceed with the refreshment: put the flour, water, yeast, and malt in the mixer, turn it on and about one or two minutes later add the Biga after having divided it into smaller parts, then pour the oil and 5 or 6 minutes later add salt and knead until the dough is smooth and detached from walls of the mixer bowl
- leave to rest covered for about 20 minutes on the workbench, then shape 260/300 grams pizza dough balls and put 8 per box
- let it ferment for about 40 minutes at R.T.
- place the boxes in the fridge at 3 °C for 12/24 hours, (remember to swap the dough box positions after the first few hours)
- before use, let the leavening continue outside the fridge for 3/4 hours, the dough must be at room temperature. before being processed

The same dough can be made by applying mass maturation. Once the refreshment is performed, folds are given and the dough mass is put in a container that will go into the fridge for 18/24 hours. The dough pizza balls will form about 5 hours before use.

The Neapolitan dough goes hand in hand with the baking temperature which must be very high, the cooking in the oven does not exceed one minute. Oven Floor temperature of 400 °C and dome 450 °C.

marana

Ingredients

- the flour used in the refreshment (autolysis) is: Italian flour type 0 W 320/350
- 56% of water (based on the total dough)
- 2,5% of salt
- 2,5% of extra virgin olive oil

Example of dough

- 10.000 gr. of type 0 flour
- 5.600 gr. of water
- 250 gr. of salt
- 250 gr. of extra virgin olive oil

Biga

- flour W 320/350
- 44% of water
- 1% fresh yeast
- 50% of Biga for this dough will be a Biga of 5000 gr. of flour, with 2200 gr. of water and 50 gr. of fresh yeast

Refreshment

- 5000 gr. of flour 0 (5.000 - 5000: let's subtract the flour used in Biga)
- 3.400 gr. of water (5.600-2200: total water minus Biga water)
- 250 gr. of salt
- 250 gr. of extra virgin olive oil

Procedure:

- prepare the Biga with the indicated doses and let it ferment for 18/20 hours at 18 °C.
- at the same time, prepare the autolysis using all the flour of the refreshment and 90% of the remaining water as well as half of the salt needed for the dough.
- When "autolysis dough" is terminated, give few folds and place it in a dough container box, cover with a lid or food film and let it rest for 18/20 hours at 18°C
- Biga and autolysis will have the same resting period and both will be put at 18 °C.
- put the Biga and the "autolysis dough" in the mixer adding the remaining salt dissolved in the water left aside, the EVO, and finish the dough

- extract the dough and let it rest for about 20 minutes on the workbench covered, after which make dough pizza balls around 200/210 grams
- continue leavening for 4/6 hours, alternatively, you can put the boxes in the fridge for further maturation

This type of dough has special characteristics due to its low pH and the great softness that comes from it.
Combining autolysis with Biga requires attention, you need to lower the total hydration desired by about two or three percentage points. The salt that we will add to the autolysis will not be the total of the mixing.

I suggest you try this kind of dough, which I find very interesting.

Ingredients

- the flour used in the refreshment is: Italian flour type 0 W 280/320
- 60% of water (based on the total dough)
- 2,5% of salt
- 3% of extra virgin olive oil
- 0,5% of malt flour (added in refreshments)
- 0,05% of fresh yeast

Example of dough

- 7000 gr. of flour type 0
- 3000 gr. whole wheat flour
- 6.000 gr. of water
- 250 gr. of salt
- 300 gr of extra virgin olive oil
- 50 gr of malt flour
- 5 gr. of fresh yeast

Biga

- Italian flour type 0 (all-purpose flour) W 320/350
- 44% of water
- 1% of fresh yeast
- 30% of Biga for this dough will be a Biga of 3000 gr. of flour, with 1320 gr. of water and 30 gr. of fresh yeast

Refreshments

- 4.000 gr. flour 0 (7.000 - 3000: total flour – Biga flour)
- 3000 gr. whole-wheat flour
- 4.680 gr. of water (6000 -1320: total water - Biga water)
- 250 gr. of salt
- 300 gr. of extra virgin olive oil
- 50 gr. of malt
- 5 gr. of fresh yeast

In these cases, it is also possible to prepare the Biga with whole wheat flour instead of putting it in the refreshment, but in this case, the Biga will not have 44% hydration but 50%, otherwise, it would be too dry. Therefore, remember to change the calculation of the refreshment.

Procedure

- prepare the Biga with the doses indicated and let it ferment 18/20 hours at 18 °C
- start the refreshment by inserting the whole-wheat flour in the mixer and adding 60% of the total water. Knead for 2 or 3 minutes and perform a 30-minute machine stop (stop & go).
- continue kneading the ingredients of the refreshment: flour, malt, water, yeast, oil, later on, salt
- after about two minutes add the Biga breaking it into smaller parts and finish the dough until is smooth and detached from walls of the mixer bowl
- extract the dough and let it rest for about 20 minutes on the workbench covered, after which make dough pizza balls of 240 grams (put 8 per box)
- leave to rise for 2 hours at R.T.
- place the boxes in the fridge at 3 °C for a minimum of 24 hours (remember to swap the dough box positions after the first few hours)
- before use, continue leavening for 4/6 hours. The dough must be at R.T. before being processed

The classic color of the whole wheat flour (also called whole-meal flour).

In this book, I have deliberately used both English and American terms for items such as flours.

Ingredients

- the flour used in the refreshment is: Italian flour type 0 W 280/320
- 65% of water (based on the total dough)
- 2,5% of salt
- 2,5% of extra virgin olive oil
- 0,5% of malt flour (added in refreshments)

Example of dough

- 7000 gr. of type 0 flour
- 3000 gr. multi cereal flour
- 6.500 gr. of water
- 250 gr. of salt
- 250 gr. of extra virgin olive oil
- 50 gr. malt flour

Biga

- flour W 320/350
- 44% of water
- 1% fresh yeast
- 50% of Biga for this dough will be a Biga of 5000 gr. of flour, with 2200 gr. of water and 50 gr. of fresh yeast

Refreshment

- 2000 gr. of flour 0 (7.000 - 5000: let's subtract the flour used in Biga)
- 3000 gr. of multi cereal flour
- 4.300 gr. of water (6500 -2200: total water minus Biga water)
- 250 gr. of salt
- 250 gr. of extra virgin olive oil
- 50 gr. of malt flour

Procedure

- prepare the Biga with the doses indicated and let it ferment for 18/20 hours at 18 °C
- start the refreshment by inserting the multi cereal flour in the mixer and by adding 60% of the total water. Knead for 3 minutes and perform a 30-minute machine stop (stop & go).
- continue kneading the ingredients of the refreshment: flour, malt, water, oil and lastly the salt
- after about two minutes add the Biga breaking it into smaller parts and finish the dough until is smooth and detached from walls of the mixer bowl
- extract the dough and let it rest for about 20 minutes on the workbench covered, after which make dough pizza balls of 240 grams (put 8 per box)
- leave to rise for 2 hours at R.T. and then place the boxes in the fridge at 3 °C for a minimum of 24 hours (remember to swap the dough box positions after the first few hours)
- before use, continue leavening for 4/6 hours. The dough must be at R.T. before being processed

You can see the seed cereals, if you don't make 240-gram loaves, it becomes difficult to shape the pizza.

Ingredients

- the flour used in the refreshment is: Italian flour type 0 W 350/380
- 80% of water (based on the total dough)
- 2,8% of salt
- 2,5% of extra virgin olive oil
- 0,8% of the malt flour (added in refreshments)
- 0,5% fresh yeast (added on refreshment)

Example of dough

- 10.000 gr of flour W 350/380
- 8.000 gr. of water
- 280 gr. of salt
- 250 gr. of extra virgin olive oil
- 80 gr. of malt flour
- 50 gr. of fresh yeast

Biga

- flour W 350/380
- 44% of water
- 1% of fresh yeast
- 80% of Biga for this dough will be a Biga of 8000 gr. of flour, with 3520 gr. of water and 80 gr. of fresh yeast

Refreshment

- 2.000 gr. of flour   (10.000 – 8.000: let's subtract the flour used in Biga)
- 4.480 gr. of water   (8.000 – 3520: total water minus Biga water)
- 280 gr. of salt
- 250 gr. of EVO
- 60 gr. of malt flour
- 50 gr. of fresh yeast

Procedure

- prepare the Biga with the doses indicated and let it ferment 18/20 hours at 18 °C
- start the refreshment by inserting the ingredients: flour, malt, water, oil, fresh yeast, and the Biga by breaking it into smaller parts and by gradually pouring the water until you reach the 65% total hydration (by referring to the example is 2.980 gr.)
- at this stage, a smooth dough must be formed, after which the salt can be added.
- now begins the critical phase of the process, before starting to pour **very slowly** the remaining water, the dough must be formed and detached from the walls tank. We must now use the second speed of the kneading machine. It is very important to have calculated the temperature of the water so as not to overheat the dough, which could otherwise collapse. If the dough does not form, you must stop the mixer and let it rest up to 30 minutes to allow the flour to absorb the water
- when the dough is well-formed, it is good to stop the machine for a few minutes before turning it on again and waiting only two or three turns of the bowl
- remove the dough from the bowl, give a few folds and put the dough to rest into a dough container box with lid or film
- we can now choose whether to put the container with the dough in the fridge at 3°C for 18/24 *(first case)* or to leave the container with the dough at room temperature *(second case)*
  - *In the first case*, it may be necessary to give some reinforcement folds to the dough, after the first hour and then put it back in the refrigerator to continue the maturation, before it can be removed for the next processing
  - *In the second case*, all you have to do is wait for the dough to double in volume, before moving on to the next processing step
- prepare the dough crates, which will be 12 cm high and not 7 cm high, sprinkling them inside with rice flour to prevent the dough from sticking
- once removed from the refrigerator, or after its doubling if at R.T., pour the dough on the workbench to move to the weighing of the loaves of dough, which will be processed and placed in pizza dough boxes already prepared. The forming phase is important and difficult because of the very wet dough, getting your hands dirty with oil helps to handle the dough, as well as using rice flours

- we make 650/700 grams loaves, the weight depends on the size of the pizza peel we prefer: remember that a too low pizza peel remains too dry, a too high pizza peel cooks badly (700 gr corresponds to a pizza peel of about 60 cm in length). The ideal would be to put one loaf dough for each box, so when the leavening is over, just turn the box directly on the workbench previously sprinkled with rice flour. If you have manual skills you can put two loaves per box, but it will be more difficult to take them or turn them over after leavening
- we stack the boxes so that they remain closed
- leave to rise for 5/6 hours to R.T. a signal that indicates the correct rising occurs when the loaves touch and come to touch the lid on boxes 12 cm high
- Once the rising process is over, the crates are turned over onto the workbench, previously dusted with rice flour. The laying is a critical phase and is done by pressing with your fingertips, keeping as much as possible the air cells in the dough that should be touched very little
- Once you've spread the pizza, you have to move it to the wooden shovel. This is a very important step because in doing so you have to remove the excess flour that is attached to the dough. Good manual skills and much practice are needed

Baking

This kind of pizza needs slow baking that favors the evaporation of most of the water present in the mixture while maintaining a very alveolated and friable structure.

- pour a little oil on the pizza before baking it
- bake in an electric oven at 280/290 °C with heat division of 60 % dome and 40% floor, for about 8-10 minutes, gradually bring the oven to 50% dome and 50% floor after some baking. (you can also try baking in a wood-burning oven but without flame and at the same temperature)
- extract the 90% cooked pizza (the Maillard reaction must not be initiated), once it has cooled down on a grid, fill it up and bake it again to finish cooking
- the second baking involves a higher oven temperature, generally between 310 and 320 °C and the duration should be about 5 minutes or end as soon as the mozzarella melts

The same dough can be cooked in a sheet pan, sheet pan pizza Roman style, in this case, the oven temperature will be: 300 °C floor and 210 °C dome, and the quantity of dough for a 60x40 cm pan is 1200 grams.

The dough that is prepared for this type of pizza is suitable for gourmet products.

Pizza loaves of 700 gr. after 5 hours of rising at room temperature.

A successful Pizza peel roman style can weigh up to 25% less than its weight before baking as if to say that 800-gram loaves once baked will be about 600 grams.

CONCLUSIONS

To obtain a perfect pizza dough, the following points must be observed

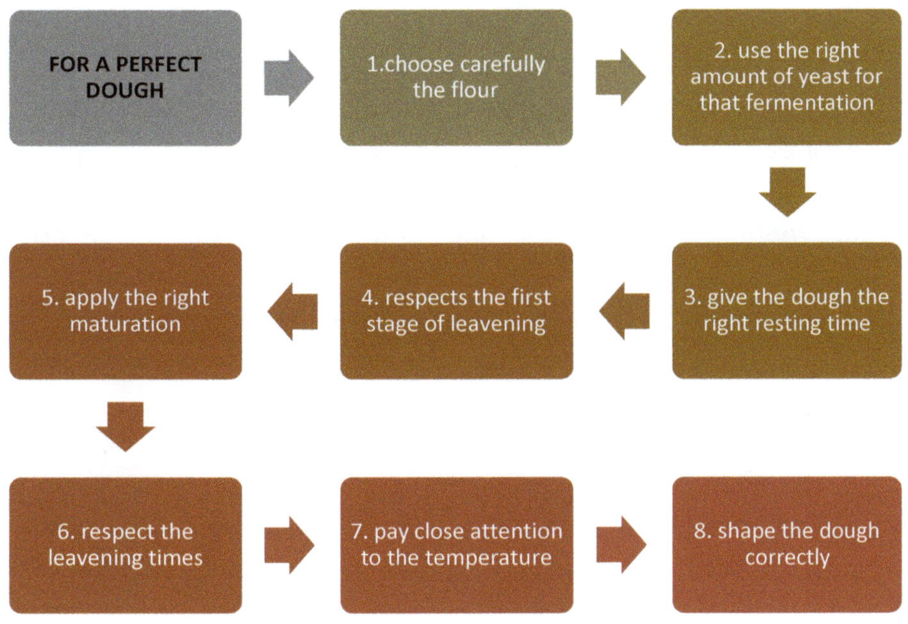

Respecting these steps means obtaining a quality product, I think it is essential to change the way of thinking when preparing a pizza, <u>you have to consider the maturation as a fundamental and essential point of the production process.</u>
let's not forget that enzymatic hydrolysis means breaking down complex parts into simpler and therefore more easily digestible

Fabrizio Casucci

Bibliografia

Adrian, J., Potus, J., & Frangne, R. (2009). *Dizionario degli alimenti: Scienza e tecnica.* Milano: Tecniche nuove.

Barbani, N. (2014). *Lipidi parte A [PDF file].* Unipi Università di Pisa. Unipi. Retrieved from https://www.unipi.it/media/k2/attachments/Prof._Barbani_-_Lipidi_parte_A.pdf

Barbani, N. (2014). *Lipidi parte B [PDF file].* Unipi Università di Pisa. Unipi. Retrieved from https://www.unipi.it/media/k2/attachments/Prof._Barbani_-_Lipidi_parte_B.pdf

Bressanini, D., & Biondi, P. A. (2012). *Profumi di acquolina in bocca! ovvero la reazione di Maillard [pdf file].* facoltà di scienze matematiche, fisiche e naturali. Milano: Università degli studi di Milano. Retrieved from http://www.orientachimica.unimi.it/Iniziative/Maillard.pdf

Carrai, B. (2010). *Arte Bianca.Materie prime, processi e controlli* (II ed.). Bologna: Edagricole-New Business media.

Casucci, F. (2017). *La Pizza è un'arte un lungo cammino verso la lievitazione del successo.* Abano Terme: youcanprint.

Cattaneo, P. (2003). *impiego del sale nella conservazione degli alimenti [PDF file].* Univerистà degli studi di Milano, Dipartimento di scienze veterinarie per la salute, la produzione animale e la sicurezza alimentare, Milano. Retrieved from

http://amaltea.vete.unimi.it/docenti/pcattaneo/AGRVET13salatura.pdf

Corsetti, A., & Settanni, L. (2007, 06 01). Lactobacilli in sourdough fermentation. *Food Research International, 40*(5), 539-558. doi:https://doi.org/10.1016/j.foodres.2006.11.001

De Vuyst, L., & Neysens, P. (2005, 01 01). the sourdough microflora, biodiversity and metabolic interactions. *Trends in food science and technology, 16*(1), 43-56. doi:10.1016/j.tifs.2004.02.012

Evans, I. D., Haisman, D. R., Sharnbrook, & Bedford. (1982). The effect of solutes on the Gelatinization Temperature Range of Potato Starch. *34,* 224-231.

Giorilli, P., & Lauri, S. (2001). *Il pane: un'arte, una tecnologia [2a ed.].* Bologna: Franco Lucisano Editore.

Giorilli, P., & Lipetskaia, E. (2003). *Panificando.* Bologna: Franco Lucisano Editore .

Gobbetti , M., & Corsetti, A. (2010). *Biotecnologia dei prodotti lievitati da forno [2a ed.].* Milano: Casa Editrice Ambrosiana.

Graw, M. (2018, 04 05). *What Are the Effects of Boiling & Freezing on Enzyme Activity?* Retrieved from sciencing.com: https://sciencing.com/effects-boiling-freezing-enzyme-activity-23207.html

Hansen , A., & Schieberle, P. (2005). Generation of aroma compounds during sourdough fermentation: applied and fundamental aspects. *Trends in Food Science & Tecnology, 16*, 85-94.

Hoseney, R. C., Zeleznak, K., & Lai, C. S. (1986). Wheat gluten: A glassy polymer. *Cereal Chemistry, 63*(3), 285-286.

MacRitchie, F. (1987, 11 1). Evaluation of contributions from wheat protein fractions to dought mixing and breadmaking. *Journal of Cereal Science, 6*(3), 259-268. doi:https://doi.org/10.1016/S0733-5210(87)80063-2

Ottogalli, G., Galli, A., & Faschino , R. (1996). Italian bakery products obtained from sourdough: characterization of the typical microflora. *Advance Food Science, 18*, 131-144.

Pacella, A. (2014). Gluten sensitivity e intestino. In a. Pacella (Ed.), *Società Idrocolonterapia III congresso Nazionale Centro Congressi CNR*, (p. 52). Bologna. Retrieved from http://www.natrixlab.it/wp-content/uploads/2015/04/antonio_pacella_slide_sict.pdf

Quaglia, G. (1984). *scienza e tecnologia della panificazione.* Pinerolo: Chiriotti Editori.

Quaglia, G. B. (2004). *Aspetti tecnologici e nutrizionali della semola rimacinata di grano duro per la panificazione.* Istituto Nazionale di Ricerca per gli Alimenti e la Nutrizione, Roma. Retrieved from http://www.ilgranoduro.it/pomb34/pdf/ottimizzazione/cap5.pdf

Quarantelli, A., Righi, F., Renzi, M., & Bonomi, A. (2003). Processi ossidativi negli alimenti di origine Vegetale. *Annali della Facoltà di Medicina Veterinaria di Parma, 23*, pp. 181-202.

Roselli, A. (2014-2015). *La digeribilità delle farine di frumento in relazione alla loro forza: sviluppo di un metodo di indagine.* [Tesi di dottorato], Università degli studi di Padova, Dipartimento di Agronomia Animali Alimenti Risorse Naturali e Ambiente, Padova. Retrieved from http://tesi.cab.unipd.it/49588/1/Tesi_FINALE_Andrea_Roselli.pdf

Shavitz, A. (2015). *impact of Sodium Chlorite on Yeast Fermentation.* [Tesi di laurea], University of Vermont, Burlinghton. Retrieved from https://www.uvm.edu/wid/writingcenter/tutortips/biolabsample3.pdf

Youcanprint
Printed in december 2023

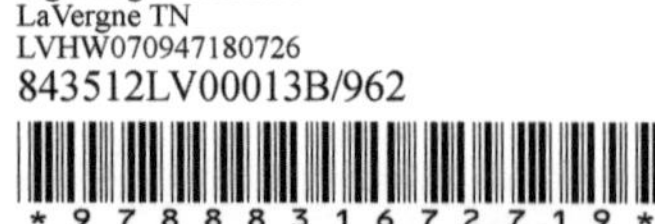
9 788883 167271